EXPLORING THE PSYCHOSOCIAL MECHANISMS UNDERLYING PSYCHOLOGICAL REHABILITATION OF ACID ATTACK VICTIMS

D1727964

Shalini Mittal

CONTENTS

Titles		Page No.
List of Tables		b
List of Figures		c
Acknowledgements		d-e

Chapters

CHAPTER- ONE

INTRODUCTION

INTRODUCTION

Sexual violence against women is not a new phenomenon. Historical documents, art and literature, stand witness to the fact that women have been coerced into sexual encounters `throughout history across the globe (Brownmiller, 1975; Zeitlin, 1986). While minor forms of sexual victimization such as sexist statements and sexually mottled whistles appear to be common, more severe forms of sexual violence against women such as rape, acid attack and domestic violence are widespread evils not only in India but also in other countries. Various forms of sexual violence are so deeply rooted in our cultures that many women who experience sexual violence often hold themselves responsible for their victimization. Moreover, many times the offenders also feel that their actions are justified by messages that convey sexual violence is acceptable. The data presented by the National Crime Records Bureau of India also show that the frequency of reported cases of sexual violence has increased multi-fold (NCRB, 2018). However, there is no way to ascertain if this increase is due to the increase in actual cases of sexual violence, or it is only due to the increase in reports of such cases. This steep rise in the number of incidents involving sexual victimization of women warrants for more and more research to gain a better understanding of this victimization of women issue, its causes and impact.

Crime

Crimeless society can be considered to be a myth (Durkheim, 1964). The problem of crime and criminals exist in all societies. The concept of crime has existed since time immemorial and is probably as old as the society itself. Durkheim (1964) had pointed out that since crime can be found in all the societies, it must serve some social function and hence can be considered to be a part of a healthy society. Durkheim

1

(1964) meant that crime serves the social function of supporting the existing social norms. It does so by setting an example of deviant behaviour that goes against the norms of society. So society comes together in the act of social solidarity and creates laws as a reaction to criminal behaviour. He further suggested that if a society operates as its usual healthy self, only a little change can be expected in the rate of deviance. Alternatively, a significant rise or drop in the crime rates would indicate a sickness in the organism. Durkheim (1964) meant that crime also serves the function of bringing about social change. When crime violates social norms, eventually the collective beliefs of the society will be transformed, thus, bringing about social change (e.g. decriminalization of homosexuality in India, removal of laws promoting racial segregation in the United States). To find a precise definition of crime is a baffling task.

The concept of crime has always been changing with the changing social conditions and is tightly knitted to the social policy of a given time. The notion of crime in ancient India is similar to the current concept of crime. Manusmriti mentions eighteen different types of legal suits that include both civil and criminal cases (Buhler, 1886). These are (1) recovery of debts, (2) gambling and betting, (3) inheritance and partition, (4) adultery, (5) resumption of gifts, (6) non-payment of wages, (7) disputes between owners of cattle and herdsmen, (8) rescission of sale and purchase, (9) non-performance of agreements,(10) assault, (11) disputes regarding boundaries, (12) defamation, (13) theft, (14) robbery and violence, (15) concerns among partners, (16) duties of man and wife, (17) sale without ownership, and (18) deposit and pledge. Kautilya (c. f. Sihag, 2009) later provided a distinction between civil law (Dramasthiya) and penal law (Kantakshodhana). Usually, all societies follow beliefs, traditions, customs and norms the infringement of which is often described as anti-

2

social. Consequently, various writers have explained crime as 'sinful', 'immoral' and 'anti-social behaviour' (Blackstone, 1765-1769, Garafalo, 1914; Gillin, 1937). John Gillin describes the crime as an offence against the law of the land (Gillin, 1937). It is an act that is harmful to the society or is believed to be harmful to the society by a group of people that is powerful enough to enforce its beliefs, and that can place an act upon the ban of decisive penalties. Blackstone (1765-1769) defines crime as an act that has been committed or omitted and thus violates a public law that either forbids or commands it. This definition, however, places a limit on the scope of crime to just actions violate public laws. Italian criminologist, Rafaelle Garafalo (1914) emphasized that crime is an act that transgresses fundamental sentiments of 'probity' and 'pity'. In the thirteenth century, the English word 'crime' referred to 'sinfulness'. However, the term comes from a Latin word crimen meaning 'cry of distress or charge'. The Latin word itself is derived from the ancient Greek word 'krima' which meant an offence against the community. Although Garofalo (1914) had linked crime to morality, it is different from sinfulness. Where sin involves a breach of morality, the crime involves a breach of law. Paranjape (2014) reviewed various definitions of crime and suggested that crime has three attributes:

1) The crime involves harm by some anti-social act of a person that the state wants to prevent.

2) Deterring measures adopted by the state are punitive.

3) The rules of criminal law procedure of the state guide the legal proceedings held for determining the guilt or otherwise of the accused.

The authors of the Indian Penal code observed that many punishable things might be less immoral than many other things that are not punishable by the law. To further

3

explain the notion, they quoted the example of a rich man who denies offering a small quantity of rice to a starving person to save him from dying. The starving man snatches and devours the rice. In this case, the rich man is morally worse than the starving man, but he cannot be punished for hard-heartedness. However, the latter is punished for theft.

Crime has been classified into legal, economic, political, social and miscellaneous crimes. Legal crimes refer to traditional crimes such as rape, robbery, theft, hurt etc. Economic crimes are inclusive of white collar crimes such as gambling, smuggling, prostitution and tax evasion. Political crimes are inclusive of politically motivated crimes or crimes committed in the violation of election laws such as willfully rejecting votes of qualified electors, altering ballots, receiving votes of people not qualified to vote. Social crimes refer to the crimes committed under social legislation such as the Protection of Civil Rights Act, 1955; Child Marriage Restraint, 1978; Indecent Representation of Women (Prohibition) Act, 1986 etc. Some other types of crimes that are committed under special or local Acts are referred to as miscellaneous crimes such as the crimes under the Consumer's Protection Act, 1980; Drugs Act, 1940; Prevention of Food Adulteration Act, 1954 etc. In India, crimes may be categorized into three categories (1) offences mentioned under the Code of Criminal Procedure (2) offences mentioned under the Indian Penal Code (3) offences mentioned under the special (e.g. Arms Act, 1959; Narcotic Drugs and Psychotropic Substances Act, 1985) or local laws or enactments such as Bhilsa Ramlila Fair Act, 1954; Bhopal Gas Leak Disaster Act, 1985 etc. With the advent of computer science and information technology, a crime of different category known as the cyber-crime has also emerged which involve the use of computers for committing crimes. Crimes under Indian Penal Code are classified into 7 categories which are (i) offences against

4

a person (ii) offences pertaining to documents (iii) offences against property (iv) offences against state (v) offences against public tranquility (vi) offences affecting mental order (vii) offences relating to public order (Information Technology Act 2000, Indian Penal Code).

Some of the essential characteristics of crime include the following:

1) Crimes have a deleterious impact on society, which may be emotional, personal, mental or social.

2) For a behaviour to be classified as a crime, it must be outlawed in advance.

3) The crime involves 'Actus Reus' or guilty action. Just the intention to commit a crime cannot be considered a crime unless it is followed by an external or overt act of crime.

4) In addition to a guilty action, a crime also involves 'Mens Rea' which refers to guilty mind or the intention to commit a crime.

5) For a behaviour to be classified as a crime, it must be prohibited by the existing penal law of the state.

6) The relation between the willful misconduct and the consequent harm should be of the nature of cause and effect.

7) For a behaviour to be classified as a crime, it must also be punishable by the state.

Victim

The term 'victim' commonly used to refer to general misfortune and has very recently been associated with the act of 'crime'. It comes from the Latin word 'victima' meaning 'sacrifice'. The Shorter Oxford English Dictionary (2007) defines the victim as 'a person killed or tortured by another'. It further continues and defines the term as 'a person subjected to cruelty, oppression, or other harsh or unfair treatment, or suffering death, injury, ruin as a result of an event, circumstance or oppressive or adverse impersonal agency.' Even though survivors of crime and their suffering has always been in the centre of attention of the writers, artists and even media portrayal, they were often forgotten by the criminal justice system until the 1970s. Consequently, many victims believed that they had fewer rights than offenders who had injured them.

Hentig (1948) suggested that in general victims include older people, young females, the intoxicated, the immigrants, the mentally defected and deranged, the dull normal and the members of minority groups. Nils Christie (1986) proposed the stereotype of the 'ideal victim' and presented the six attributes of an ideal victim. These are:

1. The ideal victim is weaker than the offender. More likely, the ideal victim will be very old or very young, a female, a sick person or a combination of these.

2. The victim cannot be blamed for what happened.

3. The perpetrator is unequivocally prominent and notorious

4. The victim is at least is doing their ordinary, day to day activity.

5. The victim is not related to the perpetrator and is not acquainted with him. (This further suggests that the offender, not a corporation but is a person. Also, the offence has occurred just once as a singular event.)

6

6. The victim can evoke right amount of sympathy in others and can, influence others in a way that he or she quickly gains the victim status without menacing (and thereby risking opposition from) strong counteracting vested interests.

However, these idealized images of victims may be different from empirical reality. Often the demographic information about the victims is derived from victim surveys. These surveys, though often helpful in our understanding of victims, can be misleading. Crimes are often underreported as the crime victim's decision to report a crime is often influenced by several factors such as gender of the victim, gender of the respondent, the severity of the crime and the relationship between the victim and the offender. In a study involving 148 respondents who informed that a family member had been a victim of a robbery, domestic assault or sexual violence, Rubak (1994) reported that only 65% of the sample advised the victim to report the crime. Also, women were more likely to advise reporting domestic assault than men. Simmons and Dodd (2003) reported that 73% of victims of domestic violence tend to be females, but 83% of victims of assault by strangers tend to be men. Research evidence also suggests that victims and offender may be from the same population, and these two categories might be overlapping. For instance, men and women who had admitted to being aggressive and committing a violent crime in the recent past also reported being victimized in the same way much more than people who had never offended (Hough, 1987; Pederson, 2001).

Nonetheless, Hazelwood and Burgess (1995) differentiated between high risk and low-risk victims, implying that some people are more likely than others to be victimized. Some victims lead a personal, social and professional lifestyle that exposes them to the risk of being victimized more than others (Hazelwood and Burgess, 1995) and are known as high-risk victims (Hazelwood and Burgess, 1995).

7

For instance, prostitutes who often walk the streets at night and would be willing to go to secluded places with a stranger for want of money and thus have more chances of being victimized.

Although the association of the term victim with a crime has occurred much recently, the concept is equally old as the concept of crime itself. Garner's (2014) conceptualization that the victim is an individual who is the target of tort or crime, clearly indicates that crime and victim are two sides of the same coin. Krishna and Singh (1982) suggested that victim could also be a collective entity such as a corporation or a whole race of the nation (for example in the case of genocide) and not necessarily an individual. A much more inclusive and broader definition of the term victim is provided by the Code of Criminal Procedure of India. According to this any individual who has incurred any loss or has suffered any injury because of the action or omission for which the accused person has been charged is a victim (The Code of Criminal Procedure Amendment Act of 2008). However, this view of victim is narrower than the international approach adopted by the UN General Assembly in the Declaration of Basic Principles of Justice for Victims of Crime and Abuse of Power (United Nations General Assembly, 1985). According to the declaration any person who has suffered any harm, including mental or physical injury, economic loss or suffers emotionally, experience substantive impairment of their fundamental rights through omissions or through acts that violate criminal laws that are operative in the member states and laws describing the criminal abuse of power.

Victims of crime could be categorized as primary victims, secondary victims and tertiary victims. This suggests the existence of a hierarchy based on the suffering experienced by the victims due to the crime. A person experiencing direct physical, psychological or financial harm due to the crime is a primary victim. Secondary

8

victims are the ones who suffer harm due to the harm experienced by the primary victim. For instance, a raped woman's children may be called bastard because of the lack of a father. Any other person, who experiences harm due to the criminal act, besides the primary and secondary victim is called the tertiary victim. For instance, in case of a terrorist attack, some people are the primary victims, and their dependents are the secondary victims. However, if the terrorists are identified as belonging to a particular community, then it garners hatred towards other people of that community. These are called tertiary victims. Abdel Fattah (2000), a celebrated Canadian Criminologist, has categorized victims of crime into five categories, which are:

1) **Retaliating Victim:** Victims of some crimes retaliate as much as possible to avoid the crime from occurring. For instance, victims of robbery and rape may not readily yield to the crime.

2) **Non-participating victims:** Certain victims are entirely innocent and cannot be held responsible for their victimization. Such victims are called non-participating victims. For instance, victims of infanticide.

3) **Provocative victims:** Some victims are provoked to commit suicide as happens in the case of dowry deaths.

4) **Participating victims:** victims of crimes like sati, several cyber-crimes and prostitution are participating victims.

5) **Latent Victims:** Some victims remain unaware of the ill effects of the criminal act. For instance, victims of blackmailing.

A similar typology of victims was suggested by Benjamin Mendelsohn (1976) based on the victim's contribution to the crime.

1) Completely innocent victims: People or children who are victimized when they are unconscious or drunk are called entirely innocent victims.

2) Victims of ignorance or minor guilt: Victims who play a minor role in their victimization are called victims of ignorance. For instance, women who may lose their lives in the process of spontaneous abortion.

3) Voluntary victims: Victims who die due to euthanasia or commit suicide.

4) Victims guiltier than the offenders: These are the kind of victims that provoke others to commit crimes and get victimized as a result.

5) Most guilty victims: Some victims commit crimes against other people and get killed in self-defense. Such victims are considered to be most guilty for their victimization.

Sexual Violence

Although crime in any form is unacceptable, one of the major concerns throughout the world is the issue of sexual violence. Sexual violence with women has been happening since ancient times, but recent incidents bring to notice that such crimes have been on the rise. According to World Health Organization (2011), sexual violence refers to 'any sexual act, attempt to obtain sexual act, unwanted sexual comments or advances , or acts to traffic or otherwise directed against a person's sexuality using coercion, by any person regardless of their relationship to the victim, in any setting, but not limited to home and work. Coercion of women to crime can embrace psychological intimidation, varying degrees of force, blackmail and/or threat (of not getting a grade/job or of physical harm). Sexual violence may even happen in cases when a person is unable to give consent, such as in cases of being intoxicated, asleep, drugged or mentally invalided.

Types of sexual violence: Sexual violence with women can take several forms. Some of these include the following:-

Rape: Rape is one of the most common forms of sexual violence. Rape may occur within marriage and in dating relationships rape or may be committed by strangers. Rapes may also be committed within families. Systematic rape is also used as a strategy during armed conflicts. Other forms of rape include unwanted sexual advances or sexual harassment, sexual abuse of physically or mentally disabled people, forced marriage, cohabitation, sexual abuse of minors, child marriage and resultant sexual intercourse, denial of the right to adopt measures to protect against sexually transmitted diseases, female genital mutilation, forced prostitution, trafficking of people for sexual exploitation and forced abortion. The Indian Penal Code of India has defined rape under section 375 as, "A man is said to commit 'rape' who except in the case hereinafter excepted has sexual intercourse with a woman under the circumstances falling under any of the six following descriptions: (a) against her will (b) without her consent (c) with her consent, when the man knows that he is not her husband and that her consent is given because she believes that he is another man to whom she is or believes herself to be lawfully married (d) with her consent, when her consent has been obtained by putting her or any other person in whom she is interested in fear or death or of hurt (e) with her consent, when at the time of giving such consent by reason of reason of unsoundness of mind or intoxication or the administration by him personally or through another of any stupefying or unwholesome substance, she is unable to understand the nature and consequences of that to which she gives consent (f) with or without her consent when she is under 16 years of age. On February 3, 2003, the definition was expanded to include same-sex crimes and the age of consent was raised to 18 years. Rapes can be of several types. These included:-

> **Stranger Rape,** where the victim does not know the offender, is known as stranger rape.

> **Acquaintance Rape** occurjs when the victim knows the offender.

> **Date rapes** are similar to acquaintance rapes as the victim may be involved in a romantic relationship with the offender. A history of prior relationship with the offender or currently being in a relationship with the offender does not mean that the rape could not occur.

> **Unacknowledged rape** refers to the kind of rape that meets the legal criteria of rape but is not identified as one by the victim is called an unacknowledged rape. Such rapes may often be mistakenly labelled as 'miscommunication' or 'bad sex' and are more common in cases of date rapes.

> **Marital rape,** also known as spousal rape or partner rape, is committed by the person to whom the victim is married or is in a live-in relationship.

> **Revenge Rape** is committed to punish a victim for their actions or the actions of their family members.

> **Digital Rape** is involving penetration with a finger.

> **Corrective rape** occurs as a result of hatred towards non-heterosexual individuals and is treated as a punishment for not adhering to their traditional gender roles.

Intimate Partner Sexual Violence: When sexual violence is committed in the form of any sexual activity by the intimate partner of the victim without her consent or any other form of sexual assault such as domestic violence, spousal rape etc., it is termed intimate partner sexual violence.

Stalking: Stalking is a pattern of repeatedly unwanted attention, contact or any other conduct directed towards a specific individual.

Sexual Harassment: Sexual Harassment refers to unwanted requests for sexual favours, unwanted sexual advances, or any other form of sexually tainted behaviour directed at an individual in the place of learning or work is called sexual harassment.

Acid Attack: the Acid attack is another terrible form of sexual violence which involves hurling acid or any other similar substance which is corrosive onto the body of another person. Until early 2013, the acid attack was not considered as a discrete offence in the Indian Criminal Law. However, after the implementation of the Criminal Amendment Act of 2013, it has been included as a separate offence under section 326A and 326B of the Indian Penal Code.

Female Genital Mutilation: It refers to the practice of removing entirely or partially the external genitalia of young women and girls for non-medical reasons. It is even considered traditional in some cultures.

Sex-Trafficking: It refers to employing, transporting, possessing, obtaining and provisioning of a person for commercial sex activities. It also involves the use of fraud and coercion to force an individual to indulge in commercial sex acts. Majority of the victims of sex- trafficking are girls and women, although, men and boys are also trafficked.

Acid Attack as sexual violence

Although a relatively new form of crime, acid attack is not as new as some people might think. Sulphuric acid or vitriol was first manufactured in Victorian Britain in the eighteenth century. Once people had easy access to it, they began using it for violent purposes in Western Europe and the USA. It became one of the most favoured weapons in domestic disputes and labour clashes. However, its use as a weapon in domestic disputes declined in Europe and the US by the middle of the 20th century. However, vitriolage (Acid Attack) gained prevalence by the late 20th and early 21st century in other parts of the world, particularly in South and Southeast Asia, Sub-Saharan Africa and Latin America. According to Patel (2014), the first reported case of acid attack in India took place in 1982.

The data compiled by the National Crime Record Bureau (NCERB) of India 83, 85 and 66 cases of the acid attack were reported in 2011, 2012 and 2013 respectively and a steep rise was noted in 2014 when the number of reported cases of acid attacks shot up to 309. The recent NCRB report (2018) suggests that there were 307 victims of acid attack in 2016. The data further reveals that 85% of victims of acid attacks are women. Another report by Acid Survivors Foundation (Acid Survivors Foundation Annual Report, 2015) indicates that acid attacks are gendered because more than 70 percent reported cases to involve women as victims. In most of these cases, women are victimized due to anger over rejection and are indicative of a tendency to dismiss any positive regard for women. As per the NCRB (2018) data, Uttar Pradesh has the highest rate of acid attacks, with 43 cases reported in the year 2014. West Bengal follows Utter Pradesh with 41 cases reported in the same year. Twenty cases were

14

reported in the Union Territory of Delhi in 2014. Other states with high rates of acid attacks include Haryana, Madhya Pradesh and Punjab. No cases have been reported in the states of A & N islands, D & N Haveli, Lakshadweep, Mizoram, Daman and Diu and Arunachal Pradesh. States with a poor sex ratio such as Haryana, Panjab, Uttar Pradesh have been found to have a higher number of acid attack cases.

Laws related to Acid Attack

Until recently, India did not have any specific law concerning acid attack. Section 326 of the Indian Penal Code, which deals with Voluntarily Causing Grievous Hurt by Dangerous Weapons or Means did not adequately deal with the acid attack because of the following reasons:

(i)   It does not include vitriolage or acid attacks

(ii) The definition of grievous hurt presented under this section fails to account for the several kinds of injuries that are caused because of acid attack

(iii) The intentional act of throwing of acid is not punished under this section

(iv) The section does not account for the planning of an acid attack, that is, the act of administering the acid attack.

(v) Also, it does not specify to whom the fine should be awarded.

Enormous discretion, therefore, was given to courts for deciding the punishment for acid attacks. Due to these shortcomings in the law, the eighteenth Law Commission of India headed by A. R. Lakshmanan presented a report to the Supreme Court dealing with the issues pertaining to acid attacks and proposed to add a new section 326A and

326B to the Indian Penal Code. The Section 326A provides that punishment of minimum ten years of imprisonment should be given to any individual who causes grievous hurt, burns or maims part or parts of the body of another person by throwing acid on them. Further, Section A puts that the punishment may be extended to life imprisonment. Also, a fine of up to rupees 10 lakhs may be imposed on the offender and that the amount of the fine shall be given to the victim of acid attack. Section A identifies the acid attack as a cognizable crime meaning and a non-bailable offence and shall be trialable by the sessions court. Further, the offence is identified as non-compoundable meaning that the complainant cannot compromise and drop charges against the defendant under any circumstance.

Section 326 B accounts for the attempt of acid attack. A person who attempts to throw acid on another individual to hurt or disfigure or disabling them shall be punishable by imprisonment of at least five years, which may extend up to 7 years. Also, a fine of up to 5 lakhs may be imposed on the offender. Attempt to acid attack is also identified as a non-bailable, no-compoundable offence. In addition to these, a presumption has been incorporated in the Indian Evidence Act as Section 114B about the guilty mind. It assumes that the person who has thrown acid on to another person has done it purposely to cause the kind of injuries that are mentioned under section 326 A of the Indian Penal Code.

The Supreme Court of India has also taken several other proactive measures. Section 357 A of the Code of Criminal Procedure states that the victims of acid attack must be given a minimum compensation of at least rupees 3 lakhs. Section 357 C of the Code of Criminal Procedure states that complete and free treatment must be provided to the acid attack victim. The section also specifies that no private or public hospital or clinic can deny treatment to the victim under any pretext and also, they must immediately inform the police about the occurrence of such an event. Any hospital or clinic, public or private that violates the legislative provisions and thereby fails to provide treatment to the victims shall be sternly dealt with under Section 166-B of the Indian Penal Code. They may have to face imprisonment for a term of up to one year, or they may have to pay a fine. In some cases, imprisonment and fine, both, may be imposed. The newly inserted section 357B of the CrPc (Code of Criminal Procedure) states that the compensation payable by the State Government under section 357A shall be in addition to the payment of fine to the victim under section 326A or section 376D of the Indian Penal Code.

In addition to these provisions to stop acid attacks and to punish the offenders of acid attack, the government also realized that acid was readily available to the public in the neighbourhood provision stores at very cheap rates of 10-15 rupees a litre and that taking a preventive measure was equally essential to curb the problem of acid attacks. So, acting on the directions of the Supreme Court, the Union Home Ministry, Government of India issued an advisory to prevent cases of acid attack and provide free treatment to the victims in addition to the compensation. The advisory also puts an immediate ban on the free sale of acid. The measures that have been imposed to regulate the sale of acids like Acetic acid (i.e. acids beyond 25% concentration by weight), Hydrochloric acid (HCI) (beyond 5% concentration by weight), Sulphuric acid (beyond 5% concentration by weight), Phosphoric acid etc. (Indian Penal Code) are:-

- Any over the counter sale of acids is strictly prohibited. If any sale of acid does occur, then the seller is required to maintain a log recording the details of the transaction. The details should include the type and quantity of the acid being sold, the address and other details of the individual to whom the acid is being sold.

- The seller can sell acid only after the individual buying acid has specified the purpose of purchase and presents a government issues photo ID.

- Acid cannot be sold to any individual who is below 18 years of age.

- The seller must declare all the stocks of acid with the Sub-Divisional Magistrate in no more than 15 days.

- The concerned SDM can confiscate any undeclared stocks of acids and can impose a fine of up to rupees fifty thousand on the seller.

- The concerned SDM can impose a fine of up to rupees fifty thousand on anyone who violates the above-mentioned directions.

Any government departments and the department of the Public Sector Undertakings, research laboratories, educational institutions and hospitals that require storing acid must abide by the following directions:

- A log about the usage of acid must be maintained and must also be filed with the concerned SDM.

- For possessing and safekeeping of acid in their own premises, an individual must be made accountable.

- All acid must be stored under the strict supervision of the person.

> Any other person, student, personnel, researcher leaving the premises where acid is kept and used must be checked.

In order to make the laws more inclusive, Section 100, which deals with the right of private defense of the body has been extended to include apprehension of grievous hurt by acid attacks. Section 100 states that an individual has the right of private defense of the body under which the person can cause voluntary death of the assailant or can cause any other harm under the conditions when (a) the assault create reasonable apprehension that it would result in death of the individual, (b) it create reasonable apprehension that such an assault will result in grievous hurt to the person, (c) if the assailant assaults with the intention of raping the individual, (d) the assailant assaults with the intention of satisfying unnatural lust, (e) the intention of the assault is kidnapping or abducting, (f) it is an assault with the intention of wrongfully confining a person, under circumstances which may reasonably cause her/him to apprehend that s/he will be unable to have recourse to the public authorities for her/his release, and (g) if the assault involves actually throwing of the acid on to the person or if the assault involves an attempt to throw acid on to the person resulting in actual harm or injury or the creation of a reasonable apprehension that it would result in grievous hurt to the person.

Causes of Sexual Violence against Women:

Several researchers have attempted to reap a richer understanding of the causes of sexual violence by explaining it from various perspectives, and several theories have been proposed to explain the causes of sexual violence against women. Some of these theories are as follows:

1) **Feminist Theory and Sexual Violence:** The first wave of feminism started around the 19th century. However, the anti-rape campaign as a part of the larger and general 'Radical Feminism' was launched in 1970, which was aimed at liberation from male dominance and patriarchy. Brownmiler (1975) is among the pioneers to explain sexual violence in terms of feminist theory. This theory assumes that gender oppression is ingrained and endemic in our society and assumes that to make sense of the world today, we must take into account the historical contexts. Moreover, the past prejudices must be examined to understand the current issues. For a major portion of the recorded history, women have been considered to be a little more than property by themselves, as well as by men (Dworkin, 1981; Clark and Lewis, 1977). Up until now, even marital rape was exempted from the law. It conveys the idea that a wife is her husband's property and thus, he is not committing any crime by forced intercourse. The patriarchal nature of our societies is at a decline, and there have been some major achievements too (Boakye, 2009). Feminists have been able to redefine sexual crimes as crimes against women rather than as property crimes (Brownmiller, 1975; Mardorossian; 2002; Roberts, 1993-1994). However, because of deep-rooted social traditions, where the men have dominated women for years, oppression has become somewhat difficult to recognize. As a result, women are often mistreated and disrespected, sometimes in minor ways. This sends a message that they are still subservient to men, and this inferiority encourages potential sexual predators to mistreat them in more serious ways.

2) **Anomie Theory and Sexual Violence:** Emile Durkheim gave the anomie theory in 1964, and it provides various explanations of crime and deviant behaviours. This theory is based on the assumption that collective conscience changes with the changes

20

in the division of labour. With the changes in society, previously held beliefs and values are rapidly questioned. As a result, traditional and modern belief systems, creating an imbalance which refers to anomie according to Durkheim. Anomie can be described as a state of 'normlessness' that further sets the stage for violence. The individuals of the state receive paltry moral guidance by this state of anomie. Consequently, the individual tends to commit a crime in order to search for stability in the environment. Historically, due to the patriarchal nature of several societies, women have to face general subordination and disempowerment (Kakar & Kakar, 2007). However, with progressive economic changes, a greater influx of women is observed in higher education as well as in the workplace. Women are no longer confined to the enclosed spaces of their houses but are now equipped with greater knowledge and skills. None the less, women are considered subservient to men in different walks of life (Trivedi, 2010). In a traditional society, the valued norm of masculinity is to safeguard women and to offer them economic security. However, since the socio-economic changes have resulted in the women being independent and in control over their own lives (Tichy et al., 2009). Men are finding it more and more difficult to achieve their masculine goals. The socio-economic independence of women seems to threaten the social structure where the joint family is valued, and the traditional gender roles are exchanged (Trivedi, 2010). Gains in financial autonomy and other social aspects of women have sprouted frustration among men. This frustration largely stems from the 'juncture of masculinity' whereby men feel that their masculinity is menaced. This further creates anomie whereby the men want to achieve a goal that is ill-formulated and unattainable. They continue to cling on to the traditional values and norms that are of little importance in the modernized society.

The men thus, try to regain masculinity by engaging in deviant and criminal behaviours of sexual violence, which mostly occur in the form of rape, sexual harassment and intimate partner violence. Chibber et al. (2012) reported that sexual, as well as physical violence by husbands, increased against women whose financial contribution to the households increased. Although the society is becoming modernized, certain aspects of it remain largely traditional due to which several evils still have a strong footing in the society.

3)   Evolution Theory and Sexual Violence: Evolution theory also explains the occurrence of sexual violence. Symons (1979) asserts that no rape can ever be completely devoid of sexual feelings. The evolutionary literature primarily talks about the adaptive hypothesis and the by-product of other mechanisms hypothesis for the occurrence of rape. Thornhill & Thornhill (1983) emphasized that rape is adaptive and occurs when men fail to compete for resources and status that would make them attractive to females. Male sexual psychology is such that they want to maximize reproductive success by varying the number of mating efforts and parental investment. According to Quinsey and Lalumiere (1995), different forms of sexual offending are modified and awry manifestations of this male sexual psychology. Thornhill & Thornhill (1983) further emphasized that a socially successful male would not rape as the cost would exceed the benefits whereas socially unsuccessful men would include rape in their repertoire as the reproductive benefits would outweigh the costs.   According to this theory, men commit rapes because it is overcompensating in terms of casual sex and no parental investment (Thornhill & Thornhill, 1983). The by-product hypothesis of rape describes rape as a by-product of other adaptive mechanisms such as promiscuity and aggression. Malamuth (1996) emphasized that although all men are capable of committing rape they do not until the relevant environmental conditions become apparent. Malamuth and Heilmann (1998) predicted that only when the possibility of getting caught and punished would be minimal, that an average man would resort to rape. This tendency to rape stems from aggressive tendencies of male rooted in the principle of 'survival of the fittest. Promiscuity is another motivating factor behind rape (Malamuth, 1996) as repeated rape would increase the reproductive benefit. However, this has often been criticized by various researchers as it opposes the feminist explanation of rape that rape is motivated by power and not sexual desire (e.g. Brownmiller, 1975; Figueredo, 1992).

4) Social Learning Theory and Sexual Violence: Burgess and Akers proposed the social learning theory in 1966. This theory proposes that people commit crimes and acquire the skills for committing crimes because of their learning occurs through the observation of the social factors in their day to day lives. Sexual violence, according to this theory, is also learned and is shaped by the consequences of such violence. If such violence is reinforced in any way, it continues and is repeated. Social learning theory explains that male sexual violence against women is modelled at both societal as well as individual level. Such behaviour gets reinforced because often it is not followed by serious punishment.

5) Broken Windows Theory and Sexual Violence: Kelling & Wilson (1982) advanced the broken windows theory of crime. The phrase 'broken window' in theory is used as a figurative expression for social disorder. The theory suggests that if a broken window in a building is not repaired, it will result in the breaking of other windows as well. This happens because the unrepaired broken window is symbolic of the fact that no one cares and severe consequences will not follow the breaking of more windows. So, the theory explains the occurrence of more serious crimes because of the disorder in the society which does not make efforts to stop crime and to punish criminals. Due to which people experience fear of crime and perceive society as unsafe. To ensure their safety in these circumstances, people tend to withdraw from the society, which further results in weakening of the pre-existing social controls. With minimal informal checks on the criminals, more serious crimes in society increase and further contribute to the existing social disorder. Broken Window theory can help explain the occurrence of an incident of sexual violence. Sheley (2018) in support of broken windows theory, suggests that there exists a cyclical relationship between appearance and reality. Existence of social disorder in the form of rape culture, support for rape myths, anti-victim attitudes and increased street harassment tends to increase the incidents of such crimes of sexual violence in the society. Because of the negative social reactions, many incidents of sexual violence go unreported, which sends out a message to offenders that little cost is involved in the act of sexual violence (Sheley, 2018).

6) **Socialization and sexual violence:** Socialization refers to the process by which people, especially children, learn how to behave in socially acceptable ways. The socialization process begins with the birth of the individual itself. Socialization of attitudes, social norms, gender roles, stereotypes and even prejudices may occur through parents, peers, teachers, significant others and media (Leaper &Friedman, 2007). There have been several researchers suggesting a link between sex-role socialization and sexual violence. Birns, Cascardi & Meyer (1994) reported a link between sex role socialization and the maintenance of abuse with the wife. Female

24

sex roles have been associated with deference (Birns, Cascardi & Meyer, 1994) whereas masculinity has been associated with more controlling behaviour (Prospero, 2008). In a study, (Prospero, 2008) reported a link between masculinity and intimate partner violence. Malamuth, Heavy & Linz (1996) proposed a confluence model of sexual aggression that emphasizes on the role of hostile masculinity in sexual aggression and proposes that sexual and power motives are the cause of sexual aggression. Malamuth (1996) describes hostile masculinity as a personality profile that involves more domineering behaviours towards women, desires to control them and misogynous attitudes. Other researchers have also tried to link evidence linking hostile masculinity to sexual aggression. Locke and Mahalik (2005), for example, found that men who conformed to masculine norms of being violent, dominating women, hating gay men and being a playboy reported more sexually aggressive behaviour. Through his script theory, Tomkins (1979) explains how hyper-masculine socialization occurs. He suggests that since childhood macho scripts favour superior masculine qualities consisting of risk-taking, sexually callous behaviour and attitudes and violence. On the other hand, feelings of fear and distress are commonly associated with females and are considered inferior (Mosher & Tomkins, 1988). Brownmiller (1975) also emphasized on the role of power motivation in the occurrence of rapes. She emphasized that in many social messages, female sexuality is identified as 'beautiful passivity' which means that women are just expected to be beautiful and passive until their 'prince charming' comes along. A lot of written literature to has often perpetuated prejudiced attitudes towards women. Famous writer Ayn Rand (1943), for example, suggested that women like being raped through her the heroine of her story 'Dominique'. Freud (1924) emphasized that women are

25

masochistic and play a passive role in coitus. He emphasizes that women crave for 'lust of pain'. A similar masochistic view of female sexuality was presented by Deutsch (1944, 1945). Through these messages, not only we have been teaching men to be sexually more aggressive, but also, we have been teaching women to be victims.

Not many people understand the causes and impact of different forms of sexual violence resulting in failure to curb such cases (Malamuth, 1996). Moreover, with the changing nature of the crime, acid attack violence has been on the rise and has long term consequences for its victims. Therefore the purpose of this research is to explore the role of psychosocial mechanisms underlying psychological rehabilitation of acid attack victims. In the following chapters, psychosocial factors that are associated with the trauma and suffering of acid attack victims and factors that can lead to effective rehabilitation of these victims are reviewed.

CHAPTER- TWO

REVIEW OF LITERATURE

REVIEW OF LITERATURE

"When women's sexuality is imagined to be passive or "dirty," it also means that men's sexuality is automatically positioned as aggressive and right-no matter what form it takes. And when one of the conditions of masculinity, a concept that is already so fragile in men's minds, is that men dissociate from women and prove their manliness through aggression, we're encouraging a culture of violence and sexuality that's detrimental to both men and women."

Jessica Valenti

Sexual violence remains a major issue universally and is linked to various psychological and social consequences that have been explored by different researchers. Several studies have explored how traumatic symptoms, psychological makeup and social support are associated with sexual violence. The present chapter systematically reviews the studies that have explored the aftermath of sexual violence and also presents various models of coping for victims' rehabilitation proposed by various psychologists. Since, very few studies have been conducted on acid attack victims, review of studies exploring the psychosocial correlates of other forms of sexual victimization have been reviewed and present here.

Sexual assault is a global phenomenon. Kilpatrick et al. (2007), have shown that about 20 million of the 112 million women in the United States, were sexually assaulted at least once during their lifetime, however, only 16% of all the rape cases were reported to legal authorities (Kilpatrick et al., 2007). Several other researchers have also suggested that the crimes of sexual assault are often underreported (Epstein &Lagenbahn, 1994; Gilmore & Evans, 1980; Gilmore, 1989; Gregory & Lees, 1996; Kilpatrick et al., 2007) primarily due to embarrassment or humiliation (Brownmiller,

27

1975; Filipas& Ullman, 2001). The FBI Uniform Crime Reports (2011) shows an extreme decline in the percentage of rapes reported to the police.

Because of this widespread rate of sexual violence and its severe underreporting, it becomes increasingly necessary to understand the sufferings and the needs of the victims of sexual violence. There have been sufficient evidences to show that in addition to physical symptoms, the victims of sexual violence suffer from a variety psychological and social problems. However, the law making authorities, legal professionals and members of society are often more concerned with the physical rather than psychological rehabilitation of these victims. Failure to acknowledge the long lasting effects of sexual victimization leads to the failure at acknowledgment of the complexity of the experiences of the victims.

Psychological correlates of sexual violence:

The scars left by sexual violence heal slowly. The consequences of such crimes manifest themselves in various physical as well as psychological problems and depending on the type and severity of the crime and other socio-psychological reasons the severity of the harm caused by sexual violence varies from person to person.

Although all victims of sexual violence may not develop chronic psychiatric disorder, the experience of sexual violence has often been associated with mental health disturbances. Women with a history of sexual violence have been found have worse mental health in terms of development of mental health problems throughout the life and also current mental health issues (Rees et al. 2011). Kilpatrick et al. (1986) reported mental health disturbances to be associated with experiences of rape and sexual assault. A study by Zinzow & Amstadteret et al. (2011) reported that students who were sexually assaulted on multiple occasions reflected poor mental health status in comparison to the students who did not have such experiences. Another study by Elkit & Shevlin (2011), reports that women who have been victims of sexual violence are more likely to be diagnosed with psychosis than women who have not experienced sexual violence. Psychological abnormalities such as generalized phobic anxiety, post-traumatic stress disorder (PTSD), depression, and substance misuse have also been reported to follow rape (Arata, 1999; Acierno, et al., 1999; Frazier, 1990; 2000; Kilpatrick et al., 1989). Severe depressive symptoms and state anxiety is also found to be associated with sexual violence (Pico-Alfonso et al., 2006). Women who were battered and raped manifested highest level of PTSD symptoms in comparison to only battered women and non-victims (Shields & Hanneke, 1983; Whatley, 1993). In addition, rape victims may also manifest intense fear of rape related situations and general diffused anxiety (Ellis et al., 1981). Rado (1948) have discussed about symptom called 'traumatophobia' in reference to war neuroses. This symptom may also be present in rape victims wherein they experience increased anxiety in settings that are similar to assault settings and try avoiding any reminder of rape. Sexual dysfunction resulting from decreased enjoyment in sexual activity due to re-experiencing of the assault may be another consequence of rape (Nadelson et al., 1982). Campbell and Soeken (1999) reported that significant correlation of number of sexual assaults could be seen with depression and body image. According to a WHO report (2013), both non-partner sexual violence and intimate partner violence have been found to cause increased substance use (such as tobacco, alcohol and drugs), PTSD, depression, eating disorders, anxiety and suicidal tendencies among victims. McCann et al., (1988) reported that nearly 20-25 % of women who experience sexual violence go on to develop long run social and psychological problems. These problems include feelings of helplessness, depression, excessive dependence, intimacy issues, loss of self-esteem and confidence. Sexual violence is also associated with personality disorders (Heard &Linehan, 1994; Herman, et al, 1989), dissociation (Cole & Putnam, 1992), increased risky sexual and drug practices (Briere&Zaidi, 1989). Pagelow (1992) reported that marital rape victims experience a cluster of symptoms similar to Battered Women Syndrome (a term coined by Lenore Walker in 1984 in the context of long term victims of domestic violence). These symptoms included poor self-esteem, depression, anxiety, feelings of humiliation and helplessness. Women who were both sexually and physically assaulted by their husbands had reported to have lower self-esteem, higher alcohol use and more negative attitude towards men than women who were only physically abused by their husbands (Shields &Hanneke, 1983). Perceived life threat at the time of the assault was found to be associated with more/ severe PTSD symptoms (Ullman et al., 2007). Kaslowet al., (1998) also observed suicide as a serious psychological effect of intimate partner violence (including both physically and sexual abuse). Other studies too have reported suicidal tendencies as behavioral correlate of sexual violence (Briere, 1992; Hilberman, 1980). A study on 2494 women of spousal violence found increased risk of suicide attempt among victims (Chaowdhary & Patel, 2008). Women who are already seriously mentally ill (SMI), experience of sexual violence tend to found to increase their symptom level (Goodman et al., 1997). Another major consequence of sexual victimization is self-blame. Classenet et al., (2005) reported that victims who experienced sexual re-victimization manifested difficulties and abnormalities in self-representation, coping, interpersonal relationships and also exhibit greater levels of self- blame and shame. Even in cases of intimate partner violence and marital rape, the victim may view the rape as her own fault (Finkelhor & Yllo, 1985).

Thus, these studies indicate that sexual violence has serious and long term psychological consequences for its victims that include increased symptoms of depression, PTSD, dissociation, personality disorders, feeling of guilt and self blame and loss of self-esteem.

Physical Health Correlates of Sexual Violence:

Besides having detrimental psychological impact, sexual violence and victimization also has several physical health consequences (Fitzgerald, 1993). Many victims of sexual violence suffer from various physical injuries, ranging from minor to more severe injuries. Koss et al. (1991) reported crime victimization as one of the Herculean predictors responsible for visits to the physician. Amar, Frederick, Gennaro, & Susan (2005) reported that among the most common physical complaints of the sexual violence victims are complaints about injuries related to busted lips, scratches, sore muscles, bruises, black eye, sprains and swelling. Victims of intimate partner rape mostly complained about having bruises, scratches and welts. However, relatively fewer victims complained about more serious injuries like dislocated joints, broken teeth, chipped teeth, fractured bones, laceration, spinal cord injuries and internal injuries Sadler et al. (2000) reported that women who had been sexually assaulted had more chronic health issues. Chowdhary& Patel (2008) have reported an increased incidence of sexually transmitted diseases among women who had experienced sexual violence. Their quality of life was also significantly low. Letourneau, Holmes and Chasedunn-Roark (1999) have emphasized on the gynaecologic health consequences of interpersonal violence. Spousal sexual violence has been found to increase the frequency of abortion and has also been associated with increased number of unintended and unwitting pregnancies (Sarkar, 2009). In a

31

study reviewing researches on intimate partner violence and sexual health, Coker (2007) reported that interpersonal violence has repeatedly been found to significantly increase sexually risk taking behaviour, occurrence of sexually transmitted diseases, sexual dysfunctions and unintended pregnancies. Victims of Intimate partner violence have also been found to report poor self-perceived health and physical symptoms (Fanslow & Robinson, 2004).

Sexual assault has also been found to be associated with restricted physical functioning and poorer general health (Golding, 1999). Increased incidences of more specific health issues are also consistently associated with sexual assault. Victims of sexual assault have often reported having chronic pelvic pains, headaches and gastrointestinal issues (Golding, 1999). Reporting similar findings Dillon et al. (2013) have shown that victims of sexual violence have increased risk of sexually transmitted infections and HIV. They also suffered from chronic pain, somatic disorders and other gynaecological complaints. Dillon et al (2013) also reported reduced functional physical health.

Sexual victimization during childhood was also found to be a predictor of more hospitalizations for illnesses during adulthood (Moeller, Bachmann & Moeller, 1993). On the basis of the review of the above studies it may be concluded that victims of sexual violence may suffer from minor physical injuries such as scratches, bruises, sore muscles etc. to more severe injuries such as fractured bones and internal injuries. In addition, victims of sexual violence may suffer from other health complaints ranging from somatic symptoms to gynaecological issues.

Social correlates of sexual violence:

The episodes of sexual violence for the victims do not end with the incident. They must inform others about her distress, escape from that situation, or move to a safe place from where she has been left (Burgess & Holmstrom, 1980). Several researches have focused on the impact of informal support system on the recovery of victims of sexual violence (Davis, Brickman & Baker, 1991; Ullman & Seigel, 1995). However, one of the major concerns in such cases is the fear of societal reactions to the incidents and towards the victims of sexual violence. In the face of unsupportive and negative societal reactions to disclosures, victims experience increased avoidance and inhibition of trauma related thoughts and memories leading to increased psychological distress (Lepore et al., 1996). In a study by Koss (1988) 42% of the participants reported not telling anyone about their sexual assault. Similarly, Koss (1985) found that more than half of the unacknowledged rape victims and around 48% of the acknowledged rape victims did not inform anyone about the incident.

As a result of sexual victimization, victims often tend to experience self-blame and stigma which include (1) recognizing of some difference in an individual based on some mark or distinguishing characteristic, and (2) devaluing of the individual as a consequence of that difference (Dovidio, Major, & Crocker, 2000). According to Goffman (1963), a stigma refers to a mark or a sign that marks it bearer as someone who is soiled, and is of lesser value than a normal person. This mark could be an inferred or perceived deviation from a norm or prototype which may initiate the stigmatizing process (Jones, et al., 1984). Several studies have reported the fear of stigma as the central reason for the rape victims to not represent themselves as victims (Koss, 1992; 1993; Groth& Burgess, 1980). Experience of rape related stigma has some prominent features (Crocker, Major & Steele, 1998). Firstly, it involves the possibility of the individual being the target of prejudicial views. This increases the

33

intensity and/or frequency of the threats to self. Secondly, it involves the awareness of devaluation of one's own social identity which poses threat to self-esteem (Baumeister & Leary, 1995). Thirdly, it involves awareness of the negative stereotypes that the other people hold about one's status. Lastly, it also involves ambiguity about being treated in a non-prejudicial manner or prejudicial manner depending on one's status. This happens because non-stigmatized people do not want to appear prejudiced or because they may be sympathizing. As a result, they may try to hide their true attitudes towards the ones stigmatized (Carver, Glass, Snyder & Katz, 1977). Major consequences of the rejection of the stigmatized individuals include social isolation and dearth of social support available to them (Miller & Major, 2000). Experiences of sexual violence are also influenced by the opinion of other people. Victims often do not accept their rape because of the fear of being blamed by others (Pitts & Schwartz, 1997).

Distress resulting from trauma may be reduced or buffered by the emotional and other support from the significant others (Thoits, 1985). Researchers have stressed on the importance of social support in the coping and improving the functioning of the individuals after the occurrence of traumatic events (Gore, 1985; Sarason, Sarason & Pierce, 1995; Thoits, 1986). Social interactions of rape victims with their spouses, family members and friends may be supportive as well as unsupportive (Holmstrom & Burgess, 1979). Researchers have reported that talking about the crime works as a therapeutic factor (Davis & Friedman, 1985). It has been found that after a traumatic experience such as rape, the discussion about the same with supportive others helps the victims to reform positive assumptions about the world, explore the personal meaning of the experience and gain control over their emotions (Janoff- Bulman, 1992; Pennebaker et al., 1990). Unsupportive behaviour on the other hand is found to be associated with poorer psychological adjustments of the victims (West, Frank, Anderson & Stewart, 1987).

Supportive responses to disclosures by the victims have been found to blunt the distress of victims and also counteract their tendency to avoid confronting the thoughts related to trauma (Lepore, Silver, Wortman &Wayment, 1996). In addition to this, cognitive and symptomatic problems have been found to be associated with the bottling up of thoughts and feelings about rape (Koss, 1988). Ullman and some others researchers have differentiated between the positive and negative social reactions and each may have independent and unique effects on the victim (Davis et al., 1991; Ullman, 1999). There are several researches suggesting that social support is related to better health outcomes among rape victims (Kimerling& Calhoun, 1994; Harvey et al., 1991; Ullman, 1996).

However, the evidences associating the health outcomes of victims to social support mechanisms are quite mixed. Starzynsky et al. (2005) claims that women disclosing about their sexual assault to both informal and formal support sources have been found to experience greater symptoms of PTSD and received more negative social reactions as compared to women who only disclosed about the assault to informal support sources. The results of another study suggested that women who disclosed about the sexual assaults to support sources got more negative social reactions than women who disclosed about non-sexual assaults (Davis & Brickman, 1996). Ullman (1996b) reported that positive social support from friends was associated with better recovery than social support from any other source. In another study by Ullman (1996c), two types of positive social reactions- firstly, allowing the victim to share about their assault and secondly, believing the victims- were found to be associated with better psychological recovery. According a study, victims who could talk to at least someone in their social network manifested lower symptoms of PTS and depression (Campbell, Ahrens, Sefl, Wasco & Barnes 2001). In the same study, two negative social reactions- firstly, patronizing and secondly, calling them irresponsible- were found to be associated with increased depressive and PTS symptoms. Other researches too have reported that negative social reactions are associated with more severe symptomatology and delayed recovery (Ullman, 1996c). In addition to these, several researches indicate that there is no relationship between social support and better health of the victims (Popiel & Suskind, 1985; Ruch & Leon, 1983; Sales, Baum & Shore, 1984).

There are, thus, sufficient research evidences to show that social stigma is associated with sexual violence victimization and cause people to negatively react to these victims. As a result, the victims often get socially isolated and may experience psychological distress. On the other hand supportive responses may be associated with better recovery of the victims. However, there are some other studies presenting contradictory findings as well.

Fear about the reoccurrence of crime:

Criminal events are essentially frightening and scary events. These are symbolic of human conflicts and raise several questions about the motivations that humans act on. Fear of crime is another, one of the most damaging consequence of victimization. Fear of crime refers to negative emotions, perceptions and attitudes about the occurrence of crime. These may include being afraid of the strangers, anxiety, concern about deteriorating moral standards in the society. According to Ferraro and LaGrange (1987), fear of crime refers to negative emotional reactions resulting from occurrence of crime or existence of other symbols that may be associated with crime.

This is the impact of crime which is not only experienced by the victim but by other people in the society who may not have been ever victimized. Although men and women both may be the victims, significant gender differences can be observed in their fear of crime. Several researches have emphasized that regardless of the place and time of measurement, women have usually reported higher levels of fear of crime (Adu-Mireku, 2002; Goodey, 1997; Lane et al. 2009; May, 2001; Softas-Nall, Bardos & Fakinos, 1995). Several researches have attempted to explain this greater fear of crime victimization among women. According to researches, women usually report a higher level of fear of crime because of their physical and social vulnerability to crime (Killias & Clerici, 2000; Skogan & Maxfield, 1981). The fact that men are physically stronger and can rape creates a possibility of real fear of victimization among women. Also, women are socialized in a manner that portrays them as weak and submissive. Hollander (2001) reported that one of the key components of being feminine is vulnerability, specifically vulnerability to violence. According to the 'shadow of sexual assault hypothesis' also known as the radiation effect, women may have a higher fear of crime victimization in general because of fear of sexual assault. This fear shadows the fear for other types of crime. In other words, any other types of crime may act as precursors to sexual assault for women culminating into a higher fear of crime among women (Ferraro, 1995; Truman, 2010; Warr, 1985). Beliefs pertaining to the severity of the consequences of crime victimization, which are more stigmatizing in cases of sexual violence, further intensify the emotional reaction (Jackson, 2009). Experience of fear of crime has several health correlates as well. According to the findings of a study by Green, Gilbertson & Grimsley (2002), feelings of safety are associated with higher scores on SF-36 predicting better mental and social health. Researchers have suggested that fear of crime tends to reduce the level of psychological wellbeing (Hale, 1996) and is associated with reduced physical functioning and poorer mental health (Stafford et al., 2007). They further reports that people experiencing higher levels of fear of crime are more likely to manifest symptoms of common mental disorders. This likelihood of reporting depressive symptoms is 90% more than those experiencing low levels of fear of crime. Limiting effects of fear of crime have also been seen on physical and social activities (Liska et al., 1988; Taylor & Schumaker, 2009). These studies thus suggest that women experience greater fear of crime because of their vulnerability to sexual violence which is associated with poorer mental health and psychological well-being.

Economic correlates of sexual violence:

In addition to harmful physical, psychological and social impacts, detrimental economic effects of sexual violence can also be observed not only immediate after the crime but also after months or years of the occurrence of the event. Due to the sexual victimization the victims' their expenditure on medical and mental health care facilities increases but because their physical and psychological health is impaired they may find it difficult to hold their jobs. Loya (2015) reported that the job of a rape victim could get disrupted in several ways including reduced performance, lack of ability to work, taking time off work and job loss. These factors lead to a decrease in the earnings of women experiencing sexual violence (Morrison & Orlando, 1999) which reduces their economic wellbeing to a great extent. Women, who are victims of intimate partner violence, have been found to spend 19% more on health care costs than women who have not been abused (Bonomi, et al., 2009). Farris, Schell & Tanielian (2013) estimated the average immediate medical cost of the victims of sexual violence to be $2084. Another study reported that women victims of sexual violence are three times more likely to drop out from school and colleges than the women who did not experience sexual violence (New York City Alliance against Sexual Assault, 2019). The financial impact of the sexual violence victimization can also be observed in the form of reduced quality of life and reduced productivity even at a national level (Waters, et al., 2004). Lost productivity of the victims and lost productivity of the offenders because of incarceration is another major consequence of sexual violence (Lawrence & Spalter-Roth, 1995). A cyclical relationship can be observed between sexual violence and poverty. Loya (2014) suggested that prevalence of sexual violence tends to be more among economically disadvantaged women. Also, the position of women who already lack access to assets and are economically insecure is worsened as lack of assets makes it difficult for victims to recover. The asset theory of Sherraden (1991) asserts that asset ownership has a cushioning effect in case of financial emergencies it addition to various psychological and physical benefits. The cost of sexual violence further involves criminal justice costs and treatment of sexual offenders (Yang, Zhang, Miller &LeHew, 2014). Other indirect costs involve loss of taxes resulting from incarceration and death (Greaves et al., 1995). Thus, there are sufficient research evidences to suggest that the economic opportunities of victims of sexual violence may reduce because they tend to drop out of schools and colleges and may find it difficult to hold their jobs. Legal and medical expenses further add to the cost of sexual violence.

Acid Attack Victimization:

Despite the existence of strict laws in India, the incidents of acid attack have been on the rise and the victims are often condemned to a life of suffering or death. In a recent case a woman police constable was attacked with acid in Mathura, Uttar Pradesh for rejecting a marriage proposal and suffered 45 percent burn injuries (Hindustan Times, April 4, 2019). In another acid attack incident, an intermediate student was attacked in her own house (Hindustan Times, May 28, 2019). She struggled for life for 38 days in a hospital following which she succumbed to her injuries and died. Another illustrative case of acid attack was that of Sonali (2003) who was attacked for raising her voice against sexual harassment (Reuters, July 28, 2012). In view of the increasing incidences of this crime and the resultant sufferings of the victims, it is crucial to understand the physical and psychosocial consequences of acid attack in order to cater to the needs and issues of acid attack victims.

Physical impact:

Acids are chemical compounds that are capable of corroding not only living tissues but also metals. Acids absorb water from the skin and react with it thereby releasing heat in the exothermic reaction. This heat damages and even causes death of the living tissues. The effects of acid attack range from redness and burns to more serious injuries which may cause death. The severity of physical impact of acid attack depends on its concentration level and also on the duration of its contact with the tissue. Acid is capable of penetrating through the skin, fat and muscles right to the bone. Sometimes it may even dissolve the bone. It can cause severe damage to nose, ears, mouth and eyes. It may completely dissolve the lips, eyelids and nostrils (Nair, 2014). Acid attack can cause temporary to permanent blindness in many cases. If inhaled, acid can cause serious pulmonary disorders. It may lead to breathing failure in two ways: firstly, it may cause poisonous reaction in the lungs. Secondly, it may cause swelling in the neck thereby constricting the airway, resulting in the strangulation of the victim. Even when burns from acid attack heal they leave behind thick scars and leave the victim disfigured in several ways. Resultant disabilities cause serious problems for victims of acid attack. With the passing of time, the scar tissue starts forming contractures thereby resulting in a need for skin grafting of the eyelids and commissural release of the mouth as they do not remain functional (Micheauet, 2004). Further, there occurs a need for physical therapy to manage restriction of movements which is itself a consequence of scarring. Also, they face daily discomfort in the form of burning sensations, severe itching and skin tightening.

Psychosocial impact:

According to Mannan et al. (2007) the psychosocial impact of vitriolage is grossly underreported. Findings of their research indicated that individuals who had experienced acid attack manifested high levels of psychological distress and were found to be high on social anxiety and avoidance. Because of the visible scars they fear social unacceptability and thus avoid social interaction. They fear staring and rejection which is strengthened by the discriminating behavior of the people (Mannan et al., 2007). They often don't get the jobs even if they are qualified for it (Yeasmeen, 2015). People either view them as aliens due to their scars or end up sympathizing to the extent of treating them differently. Consequently, acid attack victims become socially isolated and may even drop out of college and school. They may find it extremely difficult to find a groom for marriage (Nair, 2014). Victims may even find it difficult to accept themselves because of the emphasis on the outer beauty by the society (Yeasmeen, 2015).

Begum (2004) reported that most victims of acid attack violence give up their education and become socially isolated. This increases illiteracy and poverty further adding to the pool of problems of acid attack victims. Acid is used as a weapon to cause severe disfigurement to the victims and not to killing them. Maiming of their physical appearance leads to their social exclusion as they forced away from intimate relationships (Gollogly, Vath & Malmberg, 2008). Psychological impact does not limit itself to the present circumstances of the victim instead the scars remind the victim of the incident on a daily basis.

Little to no literature is available to throw light on the economic costs of acid attack victimization. However, it could easily be assumed that the economic impacts of acid attack victimization would be similar to the ones with other forms of sexual violence already discussed.

Trauma:

The English term 'trauma' comes from the Greek word 'τραύμα' which means wound. It often refers to physical injury resulting from an external force. Physical trauma can be further classified as blunt force trauma and penetrating trauma. Blunt force trauma results when a sudden external force collides with the body and leads to concussions, broken bones and deep cuts. Penetrating trauma occurs when an object penetrates the skin and causes an open wound. Physical wounds heal but often, traumatic events cause damage to the mind which renders individuals to move on in life. This is termed as psychological trauma. APA (2000) refers trauma as a direct experience of an individual of an event involving serious injury or threatened death to oneself. It may also involve witnessing some other individual being physically threatened or injured or his physical integrity being harmed.

Various events including, but are not limited to war, natural disasters, accidents, child abuse, partner battery, domestic and other fires, stranger assault, rape and sexual assault can cause trauma. Freud and Strachey (1966/1977) first expanded the construct of psychological trauma to include war, rail accidents and other sudden accidents that involved experience of fatal risks. Initial studies on trauma related symptoms were confined only in studying combat related trauma situations. But as the women's liberation movement gained momentum, researchers began to explore rape, incest, sexual assault and repression and vanquishing of women for political reasons (Lating & Everly, 1995), sexual assault and rape as traumatizing events. According to Levers (2012) traumatic events can cause not only physical and psychological damage but can also cause existential damage and spiritual damage.

Impact of Trauma:

Since long it has been identified that experience of trauma disrupts psychological well-being (Sexton, 1999). However it was not until 1980 that trauma related disorder was formally included in the Diagnostic Statistical Manual (APA, 1980). The consequent symptoms of trauma may range from acute stress disorder to post traumatic stress disorder. Acute stress disorder was included in the DSM much later in 1994 (APA, 1994). The trauma symptoms may further extend from existential crisis to other psychopathologies. Herman (1992) has differentiated between suffering as a component of existence after traumatic experience and the core experience of trauma. Core experiences of trauma are inclusive of feelings of powerlessness, terror and disconnection. 'Permanent alert' or hyper-arousal is another major symptom of trauma. Some trauma symptoms may be attributed to development of PTSD, such as flashbacks, nightmares and reliving of the traumatic event. Such symptoms are referred to as the intrusive symptoms. Another type of symptoms is referred to as constrictive symptoms as they are less readily attributed to PTSD. These may include affective disturbances such as depression, feelings of numbness and feeling detached.

As a consequence of trauma many individuals may experience disconnection with the basic human relations and feeling separated from self. This has been described by Atwood, Orange & Stolorow (2002) as the 'shattering of the experiential world'. Due to traumatic events the victims' faith and trust in the divine and natural order of the world is shattered, causing them to experience an existential crisis. Herman (1992/1997) further identified 'dialectic of trauma among untreated trauma victims. This involves cyclic patterns of shifting back and forth between intrusive and constrictive symptoms of trauma. According to Herman (1992/1997) it is crucial to identify this pattern as it may lead to misdiagnosis of the individual as suffering from either PTSD or depression, whereas the symptoms may occur for the disorders cyclically.

Another component of trauma experience is suffering. However, very little literature is available about the concept of suffering (Makselon, 1998). Suffering may have both positive and negative impact on the trauma victims and may alter the personality, level of functioning and status of health. In the long run however victims may make subjective meaning of their experiences and may contribute to their transformation from a passive victim to an active survivor. The individuals experience intrusive symptoms and numbing symptoms. Intrusive symptoms sometimes may also take the form of voluntary re-enactment. For instance, war veterans may enlist themselves as the mercenaries and rape victims may start working as prostitutes. This has been termed as traumatophillia by Horowitz (1986) and Rangell (1967).

According to a study by Breslau, Davis and Andreskiet al. (1991), the prevalence of exposure to traumatic events was 39.1% and among them 23% were observed to have PTSD. Individuals with PTSD were more likely to suffer from other psychiatric disorders, especially those pertaining to anxiety and emotional disturbances.

According to Kessler et al. (1995), experiences of rape and sexual assault increase the risk of developing PTSD among women. Kilpatrick et al. (1989) reported that women who had experienced life threat, physical injury and rape had greater incidence of crime related- post traumatic stress disorder. Findings of research by Singer, Anglin, Song &Lunghofer (1995) also suggest a strong association between exposure to violence and development of trauma symptoms. Kardiner (1941) used the term physio-neurosis to refer to the physiological and psychological components of PTSD. Riggs, Dancu, Gershuny, Greenberg and Foa (1992) compared the levels of anger among non-victimized women and victimized women, including both sexual and non-sexual victimization and indicated that victimized women expressed higher levels of anger than non-victimized women and that these higher levels of anger were found to be positively related to the development of PTSD. Hanson (1990) also reported that adult female victims of rape manifested symptoms that were similar to PTSD. Burgess and Holmstrom (1974) observed a pattern of symptoms among victims of rape which included feelings of numbness, hyper arousal, increased alertness, insomnia and dissociative symptoms. This pattern of symptoms was labelled as the "Rape Trauma Syndrome". Strong associations have also been observed between traumatic experiences and anxiety disorders (Allen, Coyne and Huntoon, 1998). Traumatic experiences also manifest high correlations with disorders like major depression (Brady et al. 2000), dissociative disorders (McDowell, Levin &Nunes, 1999) and eating disorders (Brady et al., 2000). Kilpatrick (2005) reported similar findings that mental health outcomes of violence include PTSD, panic, substance abuse and depression.

The experience of trauma may even cause psychosocial and neurobiological problems (Caffo, Forresi & Leivers, 2005). A connection has been observed between different

45

forms of dissociation and psychological trauma. Briquet (1859), formulated the concept of dissociation as a connection which was observed between the hysterical symptoms and traumatic event. Charcot (1895) too reported similar findings and emphasized on the connection between symptoms of dissociation and traumatic events. Janet (1907) observed that childhood physical or sexual abuse was followed by dissociative states. There are researches that indicate significant association of child abuse, sexual and physical abuse and other forms of traumatic events with the development of multiple personality disorder which is one form of dissociative symptom.

Other responses to trauma include inability to modulate anger and aggression and increased irritability (Kardiner; Lindemann, 1944). According to Margolin and Vickerman (2007), children who experience trauma at home are at increased risk of experiencing other traumatic events in the community. They are more likely to experience violence in other interpersonal relationships and with peers. Exposure to multiple traumas, during childhood has been found to be associated with development of PTSD and other psychological disturbances (Cloitre et al., 2009). Individuals who had experienced trauma as children are more likely to report trauma related guilt post domestic violence victimization in adulthood (Street, Gibson &Holohan, 2005). Childhood trauma has also been found to be associated with psychological problems later in life which are inclusive of, but are not limited to irritable bowel syndrome, multiple personality disorders and autoimmune disorders (Mulvihil, 2005). Findings of a research by Caffo, Forresi and Leivers (2005) suggest an increase in the PTSD symptomatology among those who report higher levels of trauma related guilt. Besides these psychological influences, traumatic experiences have been found to increase the criminality among those who experience it (Becker-Blease&Freyd,

46

2005). Eitle and Turner (2002) observed associations between traumatic victimization and young adult offending. Childhood traumatic victimization has also been found to increase the likelihood of developing juvenile delinquency (Ford, Chapman, Mack and Pearson, 2009).

It is, therefore, clearly evident in the literature that trauma resulting from sexual violence is associated with increased symptoms of depression, greater risk of PTSD and disruption of psychological well-being due to feelings of hopelessness, dissociation and terror.

Gender and Trauma:

Although both males and females can be subjected to trauma and causes of trauma might be same for both, important gender differences can also be observed in the type, prevalence, impact of and responses to trauma. Studies suggest that women experience more sexual victimization (Harned, 2001) stalking (Tjaden & Thoennes, 2000) and are more likely than men to experience trauma and injuries from an intimate partner (Bookwala, Sobin & Zdanuik, 2005; Cho & Wilke, 2010; Coker et al. 2002). Girls have been found to report, sexual assault, sexual abuse, psychological distress and physical punishment more often than boys (Tolin & Foa, 2006, Hennessey et al. 2004). Furthermore, women have been found to report a greater fear of violent male partner than males of violent female partner (Fergusson, Horwood & Ridder, 2005). Due to higher rates of intimate partner violence women have also been found to report a stronger link than males between intimate partner violence victimization and relationship dissatisfaction (Caldwell et al. 2012). DePrince and Freyd (2002) have reported that women are more likely than men to report experiencing betrayal trauma which refers to being abused by someone to whom the

47

victim may be close to or may be dependent on. Men on the other hand are more likely to suffer trauma at the hands of a stranger (Covington, 2012). It has been found that 75% of the offenders of domestic violence are males (Snyder & McCurley, 2008).

Due to the differences in the experience of trauma, the effects of such trauma are also different (Covington, 2012). Both boys and girls responses to trauma involves feelings of anger and dissociation. However, girls more frequently suffer from anxiety and depression (Foster et al. 2004), and are more likely to suffer from PTSD than boys (Abram et al. 2004). In a study Berg (2006) measured PTSD, subjective experience of sexism and checklist of gender based stressors which were inclusive of violent acts. Moderately strong correlation was observed between sexist experience and PTSD. Also, sexist degradation was found to be a predictive variable for trauma. DePrince and Freyd (2002) reported that betrayal trauma is linked with poorer mental health outcomes including PTSD, depression and anxiety. In several cases of sexual abuse re-traumatisation may also occur for girls due to practices that involve body searches, physical examinations, forced disrobing and restraining of the girls to beds or restraining by male staff members (Ford et al. 2007; Hennessey, 2004).

Glick and Fiske (1996, 2001) proposed the theory of ambivalent sexism that suggests that social sexism has two components namely hostile sexism and benevolent sexism. Hostile sexism refers to overtly attributing humiliating and negative characteristics to women. Benevolent sexism on the other hand is relatively subtle and involves attributing subjectively positive statements to women but which are degrading and harming for the gender. Glick et al. (2002) reported that men's hostile sexism is predictive of aggressive behaviour towards females. Men who are high on hostile sexism are not only more likely to physically and sexually aggress against women, but

48

are also more likely to hold positive views about beating wives and blame women for their abuse. Hostile sexism by men has also been found to be predictive of rape myths among them. Benevolent sexism attempts to offer females protection as long as they remain in subservient positions to men and follow traditional gender roles. Benevolent sexism has been found to disarm women thus increasing their vulnerability to violence. Squeals of victimization such as Battered Women Syndrome and Rape Trauma Syndrome are also be experienced by female victims and not by male victims. Burgess and Holmstrom (1974) coined the phrase Rape Trauma Syndrome referring to psychological, behavioural and physical symptoms that are experienced by rape victims. These symptoms are grouped into acute phase and long term reorganization phase. The acute phase begins immediately after the incident of rape and may last upto 2-3 weeks. This phase may involve physical consequences for the victim in addition to strong emotional responses. Emotional response may involve an 'expressed emotional style' (i.e. fear, anxiety, crying, laughing etc.) or a 'controlled emotional response' (i.e. flat affect, calm etc.). The long term reorganization phase involves attempts to reorganize one's life and may persist from six months to over a year. This reorganization may be adaptive or non-adaptive. During this phase the victim may attempt to lead a normal life by relocating to a new residence or seeking social support from family and friends. In many cases they may even develop intense fear of being attacked again and traumatophobia.

Walker (1984) coined the phrase 'Battered Women Syndrome' which refers to clusters of behavioural and psychological symptoms experienced by victims of prolonged intimate partner violence. She suggested that spousal abuse in cyclical in nature and involves the tension building stage, acute battering incident and the stage of loving contrition. She also suggested that experiencing the cycle just once also may result in development of symptoms of Battered Women Syndrome which are similar to the symptoms of PTSD. The symptoms involve feelings of depression, anxiety, hopelessness, isolation, sleep disturbances, intrusive thoughts and feelings about the abuse among other symptoms.

Caldwell et al. (2012) proposed that because of cultural factors male gender is ascribed a higher status than female gender. Consequently, females experience contextual factors that result in their disempowerment and increase their risk and experience of sexual abuse. It is, therefore, obvious from the literature that both males and females can experience trauma but they differ in terms of the kind of trauma experienced and manifestations of symptoms.

Models of Coping with Trauma:

Several models have been proposed by psychologists to explicate the process of victimization and consequent attempts to cope. Some of these models have been reviewed here.

Levison's coping model: This model is proposed by Casarez Levison (1992) for victims. The model sheds light on the individual's pre crime state and follows the individual from that stage to the time of the crime, the immediate aftermath of the crime, early coping and finally to the stage of reorganization. The model enumerates the following stages of coping of the victims.

Pre-victimization (Organization)- This stage sheds light on the level of adaptation of the victim as it was prior to the victimization. In other words it focuses on the individual's way of dealing with the daily stressors of life before he/she was victimized. Here, the focus is not only on the psychological resources of the individual but also on the personal, economic and social resources.

Victimization (Disorganization)- The second stage is the stage of disorganization and focuses on the event of victimization itself (the crime). The emphasis is on the state of the victim from the initial few hours of victimization up to couple of days after the event of victimization. During this stage the victim may experience physical or psychological injury, disorganization and traumatic stress. In addition to this they may also experience hopelessness, helplessness, anger, disbelief and shock.

Transition (Protection)- During the transition stage the victims try to cope with their circumstances. They need social support from various professional and social networks in order to cope in a better way and to reach the stage of reorganization. However, in the cases where the victims use maladaptive coping strategies, the victims will fail to cope appropriately and reach a stage of total exhaustion.

Reorganization (Resolution)- The stage of reorganization does not involve returning the victim to the level of functioning that existed prior to the victimization. The stage of reorganization occurs when the victim incorporates an understanding of his/her traumatic event into his/her understanding of him/herself in relation to the world. This enables restoration of the victim to a normal state of functioning where they may return to daily life routine and normal relations. Individuals may differ in the time required to reach this stage. Some victims may take 10-12 months to start functioning normally while others may take years.

Transtheoretical Model of Change: The Transtheoretical Model of Change proposed by Prochaska, DiClemente and Norcross (1992) suggests that different individuals react differently to the violent experience and hence have different needs after the violent experience. Thereby, this model emphasizes on providing focused intervention to each individual as per his or her needs. The model emphasizes to determine the level of services required by the victim which may range from merely sharing of information to providing intensive individual therapy. The model further emphasizes that the focus should not only be on the primary victims but also on the society and the victim's support network. This will enable the victims to evaluate their situation more quickly and reduce the distress caused due to a need for search of new resources. The steps involved in this model are following.

Educating the victim: Victims must be educated about the process of coping with trauma. They should be well informed about the procedures of criminal justice system, about the professionals looking into their case and about their respective roles in the case. Victims should also be given knowledge about the goals as well as the process of therapy so as to enable them to make informed choice. To serve this purpose, pamphlets, booklets and information seminars may be utilized.

Educating the Support System: People who form the part of the victim's support system, must be educated so that they are more efficient at providing the appraisal, informational and emotional support to the victims. This can be achieved by training them on how to respond to their partner or friend's victimization experience. This can also be achieved by providing a better understanding of the traumatization process and the reactions that the victims can possibly give.

Peer Support Groups: Some victims may not need professional help. Therefore in such cases peer support groups turn out to be very helpful as well as cost-effective. However, such groups must be linked to some professionals so that the victims can easily access them if the need arises.

Professional Support Groups: In case of victims who are more severely traumatized, support groups that are professionally supervised tend to prove more helpful. The professional support groups enable the victims to build up strength and prepare them for more active and intense treatment programmes.

Therapy: Therapy can prove extremely beneficial for victims who are severely traumatized. The professionals are able to identify the trauma symptoms and then assess the individual needs of the victims. Thereby, they can provide therapy that is best suited to the individual victim. Depending on their requirement, the professionals may decide on long-term intervention or the short-term intervention.

Paraprofessionals: There are several paraprofessionals that work in the field of victim services. These paraprofessionals too examine the victims and help in providing interventions that may improve the condition of the victims. They may also help the victims in identifying their own problematic reactions that may hinder their successful and complete recovery.

Scott, Oberst and Dropkin's Coping Framework: In 1980, Scott, Oberst and Dropkin provided a coping framework which emphasized on five tasks that are required for psychological recovery of traumatized victims. The five tasks are:

Mourning the loss: The first task in the process of psychological recovery is to mourn the loss. Embracing the seriousness and severity of the loss must be comprehended completely and fully.

Confront the loss: The next task is to deal with the loss by facing the problem and not running away from it.

Confront the possible denial: The next task is to identify the different forms of denial that the victim may manifest and deal with them.

Reframe the experience: In the next task the victims must redefine their victimization experience. They must acknowledge the loss suffered but at the same time they must find hope and mastery in the skills newly found.

Integrate the experience: The final task is to incorporate and integrate their victimization experience, their disfigurement and other trauma symptoms into their overall self-concept.

Sexual violence and Psychological Makeup:

Psychological makeup can be defined as the emotional constitution of an individual that causes reactions and motivates the actions of the individuals. Researches in this area have reported a number of factors that are related to individuals' psychological makeup, which further have an influence on their experience of sexual violence. Studies suggest that sexual victims may engage in guilt or self-blame under the influence of rape myths, especially if they feel that they could have prevented their victimization (Giacoppassi & Dull, 1986). Janoff Bulman (1979) suggested that self-blame is of two types, behavioural self-blame and characterological self-blame. Behavioural self-blame pertains to actions that can be controlled and is adaptive in nature. On the other hand, characterological self-blame pertains to feelings of worthlessness and is maladaptive in nature. Finkelson and Oswalt (1995) reported that victims tend to internalize blame if they feel that people will judge their experience negatively. The researchers have often debated over the role of self-blame in trauma experiences. Janoff-Bulman (1979) reported that development of self-blame was found to be associated with enhanced feelings of control among some victim. As per this hypothesis, victims who blame themselves for sexual violence may be able to cope in a better way as long as the blame is pointed at controllable and specific behaviours. This behavioural self-blame may be related to better adjustment and coping because the victims feel that they can change those specific behaviours and avoid being victimized in the future (Frazier, 1990). Characterological self-blame, on the other hand, is attributed to uncontrollable and stable aspects of the self. So, characterological blame does not enhance a sense of control and is considered to be maladaptive (Frazier, 1990).

Another aspect of psychological make-up that may influence the coping process of the victims is self-efficacy. It refers to the perception that an individual will be able to initiate and carry out a coping strategy (Bandura, 1997). Being able to believe that one has control over his/her situations and over reducing his/her distress, increases the likelihood of utilizing the available coping resources after the trauma experience (Ross & Mirwosky, 1989). High perceived control has been found to be associated with increased possibility of risk seeking (Norris, Kaniasty & Scheer, 1990).

Another aspect of psychological make-up often associated with sexual violence is hopelessness. Several studies indicate that feelings of hopelessness are commonly experienced by victims of sexual violence (Scher & Resick, 2004). Hopelessness has been found to increase suicidal intent (Dyer & Kreitman, 1984) and has also been found to predict suicide attempts and suicide completion (Kuyken, 2004).

Thus, the literature suggests that sexual violence leads to development of a psychological make-up that perpetuates pathological states and that altering psychological make-up may help in improving the level of functioning of an individual.

CHAPTER- THREE

RATIONALE, OBJECTIVES AND CONCEPTUAL FRAMEWORK

Rationale:

With the starting of the second wave of feminism in the early 1960s, an emphasis was made on the cultural and social inequality between the male and female genders and the resultant sexual violence. Issues of domestic violence, rape and sexual violence were brought to the forefront of feminist discussions. Beauvoir (1949) in her book the 'The second sex' described the males as the default and women as the 'other'. Feminist researchers such as Brownmiller (1975) and Beauvoir (1949) rejected authors like Sigmund Freud, Ayn Rand and Friedrich Engels who portrayed females as the subservient gender associated it with sexuality. In Freud's famous psychoanalytic theory, even the pious relationship of a mother and child did remain untouched by sexuality. On one hand sexuality has been found to evoke intimacy and identity on the other hand it has also been found to evoke sexual violence.

Throughout history women have been coerced into sexual encounters and have been at the receiving end of sexual violence in one form or another. As discourse on rape, marital rape and other forms of sexual violence gathered momentum during the second wave of feminism several researchers focused their attention on understanding the impact of such sexual violence (for example: Hilberman et al., 1980; Finkelhor & Yllo, 1985; Kilpatrick et al., 1988; Amar et al., 2005; Kilpatrick, et al., 2007). The issue of sexual violence against women is so deeply rooted in our society that many of the time it is not even noted as crime. The discourse of #MeToo also sheds light on the extent to which the issue of sexual violence is prevalent.

However, the review of literature presented in the second chapter sheds light on some major gaps in literature related to sexual violence, resulted trauma and the rehabilitation process and outcomes. First, very few researches have attempted to explore the aftermath of acid attack (Begum, 2004; Mannan et. al., 2006; Yeasmeen, 2015). Despite the fact that the first case of acid attack occurred in India in 1920, until recently it was not even recognized as a separate offence (Criminal Law Amendment Act, 2013). Consequently, acid attack victims are grossly underrepresented in media and literature.

Second, Despite the steep rise in the number of acid attack cases over the years, the talks of rehabilitation of acid attack victims mostly revolve around ensuring that their offender is punished, that the victims get a proper treatment primarily for their physical injuries and victim compensation under section 357 A. However, not much is known about the factors that contribute to the psychological rehabilitation of the acid attack victims. It is noted in the literature that in case of acid attack the physical impact is much severe and the damage is permanent. Also the damage is to an aspect which is closely related to their identity. Here their own face becomes a constant reminder of the crime that happened with them. This incidence of sexual violence, therefore, sample is very different from other forms of sexual violence as the damage is permanent which may lead to re-occurrence of the trauma associated with the crime. The rehabilitation is such cases need to be carefully designed and must involve both the professionals as well as members of victim's family and support group. Therefore, it becomes very crucial to understand the needs and issues of acid attack victims and the factors that can contribute to their long term psychological rehabilitation.

Objectives of the present Research:

Based on the review of literature and above mentioned gaps in the literature, the present study was planned to understand the needs and issues of the victims of acid attack. It also intends to understand role of resulted trauma and psychological makeup in the psychological rehabilitation of acid attack victims. An important objective of the research was also to understand the role of social support in the psychological rehabilitation of victims.

The research strategy:

Considering the exploratory nature of the study and psychological sensitivity of the victims of acid attack, a mixed method approach was adopted for the present study. It involved a quantitative survey of variables found to be relevant in cases of sexual violence and an in-depth qualitative analysis using victims' narratives about their experience pre, during and after the incident.

Conceptual framework of the study:

The present study utilizes the Psycho-social Coping Theory proposed by Dussich (1985). The purpose of the theory is utilitarian and explanatory and it attempts to improve our understanding of all forms of victimization and facilitate the recovery process of the victims. It suggests that coping is inherently adaptive and even creative in nature. It focuses on the purposive usage of the available resources. The Psycho-social Coping Theory (PSCT) describes the process by which people deal with their victimization and thereby reduce stress. The scope of PSCT is dynamic, behavioural and comprehensive. The Problem, the Repertoire, the Coping Processes and the Products are the major elements in PSCT. The Problem refers to the situations that disturb the equilibrium of the individual. These serve as the inputs in the coping model. The Repertoire refers to the problem solving skills of an individual which he/she may utilize in order to deal with the stresses of life. The Repertoire is composed of the individual's physical, psychic, and social assets and is supported by time. The Coping Process involves four elements in the sequence of Prevention, Preparation, Action and Reappraisal. The Coping Process results in the reduction or complete elimination of the stress or retention of the stress (Dussich, 2006). The coping model based in Psycho-social Coping Theory is discussed in detail below.

Psycho-social coping model:

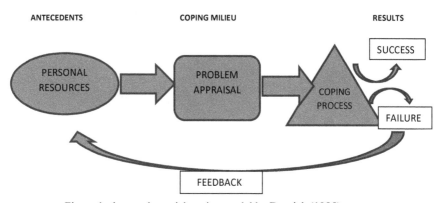

Figure 1: the psychosocial coping model by Dussich (1985).

Dussich (1985) has proposed the psycho-social model of coping which utilizes both legal and behavioural concepts to provide an understanding of various forms of victimization and expedite the recovery process of the victims. The model proposes that each individual has a coping environment within which he tries to cope. This is called as coping milieu. The coping milieu consists of the social, physical and psychic interactive space and differs from person to person and problem to problem.

The model entails that each individual has personal resources that consist of his/her social assets (such as social role, sibling position, social class etc.), repertoire (behaviour or skills that a person habitually uses), physical assets, psychic assets (such as personality, skills, education, intelligence etc.) and time. The individual utilizes these personal resources to confront the problem within the milieu. So, the P/SCM (psycho-social coping model) begins with coping milieu and the 5 resources of the individuals which are given below.

PERSONAL RESOURCES

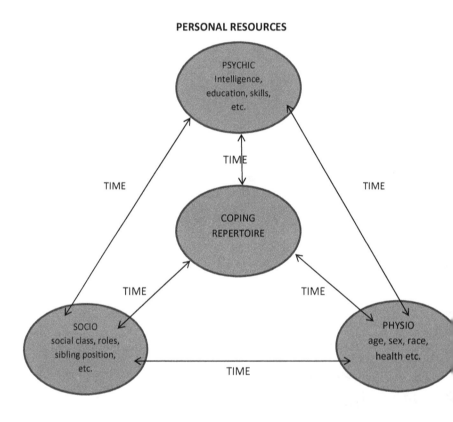

Figure 2: the personal resources of an individual and the relation among them.

Numerous continua constitute each problem and they are evaluated by the individual at a given point in time. The time required by the individual to assess and evaluate the problem is known as 'problem freeze'. In other words, problem freeze is a heuristic that enables an individual to freeze time in order to evaluate each continuum. The various continua evaluated during the problem freeze include time continuum (duration of time for which the problem has persisted), due continuum (time available for the resolution of the problem), evolution continuum (the pace at which the problem became apparent), person continuum (number of people involved in the problem), severity continuum (the extent to which the problem is complex), threat continuum (the extent to which the well-being of the individual is threatened, familiarity continuum (the extent to which the person is familiar with the problem and context continuum (the extent to which the problem lies within or outside the context).

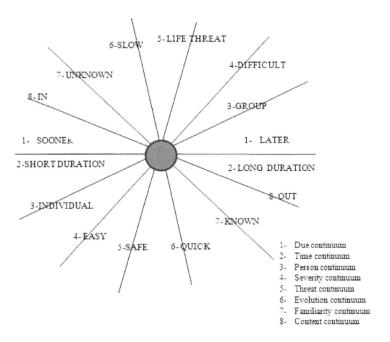

Figure 3: the Problem Freeze Continua Tool

The psycho-social coping consists of four phases. Each phase is a continuum within which the individual can make choices with success being at one end and the failure being at the other end. It begins with the phase of prevention which involves awareness that a problem might be possible. During the phase of prevention, denial of the problem is likely to cause failure and reasonably accepting problem will lead to success. The second phase is known as the preparation phase. This involves awareness of the fact that the problem is impending. This awareness will lead to the person worrying, appraising, practicing and rehearsing. This behaviour might lead to success. On the other hand the absence of these behaviours will lead to failure. The third phase is the action phase which commences when the problem presents itself. The individual may be able to cope successfully in the face of the problem if they are able to utilize learned resourcefulness, self-delivered reassurance and diminished vulnerability. On the other hand the individual will fail to cope due to learned helplessness, increased vulnerability and disappointment.

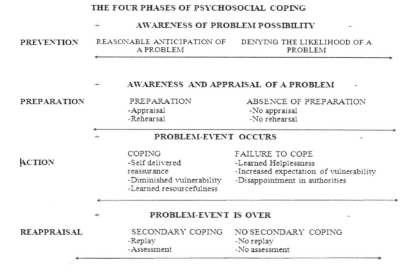

THE FOUR PHASES OF PSYCHOSOCIAL COPING

	← AWARENESS OF PROBLEM POSSIBILITY -	
PREVENTION	REASONABLE ANTICIPATION OF A PROBLEM	DENYING THE LIKELIHOOD OF A PROBLEM

	← AWARENESS AND APPRAISAL OF A PROBLEM -	
PREPARATION	PREPARATION -Appraisal -Rehearsal	ABSENCE OF PREPARATION -No appraisal -No rehearsal

	← PROBLEM-EVENT OCCURS -	
ACTION	COPING -Self delivered reassurance -Diminished vulnerability -Learned resourcefulness	FAILURE TO COPE -Learned Helplessness -Increased expectation of vulnerability -Disappointment in authorities

	← PROBLEM-EVENT IS OVER -	
REAPPRAISAL	SECONDARY COPING -Replay -Assessment	NO SECONDARY COPING -No replay -No assessment

Figure 4: The phases of psychosocial coping

The last phase is the phase of reappraisal which commences when the problem ends. During the phase, secondary coping will occur due to replay and assessment. The absence of which will lead to absence of secondary coping.

The psycho-social model of coping can be applied to victimization and recovery and contribute to our understanding of the process. During victimization, the individual is unable to cope with the attack on her/ him because s/he does not have the adequate resources. The end- state is the recovery which occurs when the victim returns to a functional lifestyle whereby the individual adopts a positive identity and has considerably fewer symptoms. As a result of inadequate resources the individual experiences vulnerability, victimization and a reduced ability to recover. On the other hand, as a result of adequate resources the individual experiences resiliency, safety and improved ability to recover. Based on this psychosocial coping model the following victim taxonomies have been developed:

1. **Pre-victimization:** Individuals in vulnerability conditions such as distorted problem appraisals, social disability, faulty coping, limited time etc., experience increased vulnerability and hence are at a higher risk of getting victimized.

2. **During victimization:** Individuals who utilize techniques such rational action, positive thinking, problem solving, self-delivered reassurances have a greater likelihood of coping (Dussich, 1988).

3. **General post-victimization:** Victims with adequate personal resources are able to enhance their coping and recovery. On the other hand, victims who have inadequate resources engage in maladaptive coping and continue their suffering.

4. **Specific post-victimization:** Individuals with resiliency conditions such as physical strength, appropriate coping, time abundance, positive intervention etc., have greater chances of recovering from their victimization.

The psycho-social model of coping is used to gain a better understanding of the behaviours of the victims regardless of how they were harmed (Holley & Brewster, 2006). It also assists in their recovery. The model emphasizes on the importance of the holistic multi-resource approach to understanding victimization and subsequent recovery. Since the model suggests that lack of resources increases likelihood of victimization, recognition of the resources that are lacking can contribute in prevention of victimization. Individually tailored resources which are specific to the individual and are culturally specific and realistic can not only prevent victimization but also help in recovery. Appropriate coping methods may be taught in order to facilitate recovery. These coping skills may be the ones never taught to them earlier at homes. One of the most important skill being that of problem solving which involves assessing the problems realistically, searching for alternative solutions on the basis of their outcome, choosing the best possible options and evaluating the resultant outcomes.

The psycho-social coping model is a holistic multi-resource model suggests that when a problem presents itself, the victim evaluates it along numerous continua and tries to cope with it within the coping milieu. Availability of adequate resources improves a person's ability to recover. Thus, regardless of how an individual was harmed, the psycho-social coping model improves our understanding of how victims behave and cope. Therefore, this model serves as the conceptual framework for this study.

CHAPTER- FOUR

METHOD

METHOD

The preliminary fieldwork:

In order to gain understanding of the nature and prevalence of sexual victimization and to gain sensitivity required for undertaking the present study a preliminary fieldwork was carried out with the help of a NGO named DISHA (Developing Intervention for Social Human Action). The preliminary fieldwork involved narrative interviews of 17 rape victims (all females) and their family members, 2 sexual offenders and Judicial Magistrates residing in rural district of Amravati, Maharashtra. The analysis of the narratives using Thematic Content Analysis revealed that victims of such crime belong to diverse age groups. There were themes related to social stigma, fear of crime and guilt. In several cases it was also observed that re-victimization of the victims occurred due to the prejudiced attitudes of the society as well as their family members. This even resulted in social isolation of the victims in many cases and dropping out from schools and colleges. Interaction with the Judicial Magistrates also revealed that more often than not, victims were not aware of the legal proceedings and hence felt helpless. Also, often victims of crime were reduced to the roles of mere witnesses and often had no one to cater to their psychological issues.

The preliminary fieldwork not only highlighted the issues faced by the victims of sexual violence such as fear of crime, stigma, lack of emotional and informational social support, but also helped in the sensitization of the researcher towards the victims. Although, the preliminary fieldwork was not carried out on acid attack victims, it contributed to the understanding of the victimization experience because all forms of sexual violence tend to have similar impact.

The Mixed Method Approach:

The present research adopted a mixed method approach which involves collecting, analyzing and mixing qualitative and quantitative data in a single study. Mixed methodology is based on the premise that a combination of quantitative research (variable oriented research) and qualitative research (person oriented research) would provide a better understanding of the research problem than either of the research methods alone (Creswell & Clark, 2011). The concept of combining qualitative and quantitative data was first introduced by Jick (1979) in the purview of organizational research. Qualitative methodologies provide a micro view of the problem and involve holistic and naturalistic collection of data thus providing a rich descriptive data. Qualitative data is in the non-numeric form (words, narratives, and descriptions) and are generated through interviews, focus groups etc. Quantitative data on the other hand is in numeric form and provides a macro view of the problem. Quantitative researches involve pre-determined and instrument based questions. The integration of these two different methodologies is called mixed methodology and the two types of data can be combined at varying points and in different ways in the research process (Creswell, 2009). Testa, Levingston, VanZile-Tamsen & Frone (2011) emphasize that any area of study can be benefitted from the use of mixed methods.

Benefits of Mixed Methods:

In support of the usage of mixed methodology, Jick (1979) noted that it enables the researchers to be more confident of their findings, leads to the development of more creative ways of collecting data, provide richer data, reveal contradictions and lead to integration of theories. Denzin (1989) emphasized that mixed methods enables to cancel out bias inherent in any particular source of data. Greene et al. (1989)

identified complementarity, triangulation, initiation, development and expansion as the rationale for the usage of mixed methods. Rossman & Wilson (1994) also emphasized that combining qualitative and quantitative research methods allow for confirmation and corroboration of each other. Complementarity, additional insight, increased validity and pushing the research further were identified by Rank (1999) as the benefits of using mixed methods. Since the advantages and disadvantages of qualitative and quantitative researches are pretty much opposite to each other hence they complement each other by "mutually supporting each other's lacking" (Webster, 1974). Mixed methods also provide an additional insight into the way the respondents view and interpret the world, theoretical perspectives and methodological approaches. Consistency of results with qualitative and quantitative methods serves to validate the data and enhance the confidence of the researchers in the findings of their study. Integrating qualitative and quantitative methods sometimes reveals discrepancies that provide richer data, greater insight and potential to redirect inquiries.

Although various sophisticated quantitative studies have attempted to explore the various aspects of women victimization (Kilpatrick et. al. 2007; Mittal et. al. 2017; Prospero, 2008) and several qualitative researches have also provided an insight into the subjective experiences of victimization (Leiting & Yeater, 2016; Igras et. al. 1998), mixed method researches must be carried out for the best and holistic understanding of violence against women (Murphy and O'Leary, 1994).

Participants:

The present research utilized homogenous purposive sampling which focuses on recruiting participants that share specific characteristics. A total of 30 female victims of acid attack residing in the state of Uttar Pradesh participated in the study. All the victims belonged to lower and middle socio-economic status and they had basic education. All the victims were young adults and belonged to the age group of 18 to 25 years. Out of the total of 30, 14 victims were married at the time of the incident of acid attack and the rest were unmarried. Three victims got married during the course of the research.

Measures:

For the quantitative analysis the following tests were used for the collection of the data:

1) *Beck Depression Inventory- Hindi:*

The severity of depressive symptoms was measured using Beck Depression Inventory (Beck, 1961)). It is a multiple choice self-report inventory consisting of 21 questions. For the present study, the Hindi translation of the inventory by Prashant (1988) was used. The responses are scored on a scale of 0-3 where higher scores are indicative of more severe depressive symptoms. The content validity of BDI-H is .67 and Cronbach Alpha is .84. It can be used with respondents 13 to 80 years of age.

2) *Positive and Negative Affect Schedule- Hindi*

Watson, Clark and Tellegen (1988) originally developed PANAS (Positive and Negative Affect Schedule) to obtain a measure of positive and negative affect. The Hindi version of the test was developed by Pandey and Srivastava (2008). The scale consists of 10 items for measuring positive affect and 10 items for measuring negative affect. The reliability for the positive affect and negative affect subscales and for the full scale are found to be .80, .78 and .66 respectively. Responses are scored in a scale of 1(very slightly or not at all) to

5 (extremely or always). To obtain a score for positive affect scores on items 1, 3, 5, 9, 10, 12, 14, 16, 17, and 19 are added. Higher score is indicative of higher level of positive affect. To obtain a score for negative affect 2,4,6,7,8,11,13,15,18 and 20 are added. Lower scores are indicative of lower level of negative affect.

3) *General Health Questionnaire- Hindi*

General Health Questionnaire (GHQ) was originally developed by Goldberg and Hollies (1979) as a screening device for identifying psychiatric cases in the population. The original questionnaire consisted of 60 items. GHQ was adapted for Indian population by Singh (2000). GHQ 28 is the shorter version of scale having 28 items to be rated on 4 point rating scales. The GHQ 28 is used to assess four dimensions of general health problems namely anxiety/insomnia, depression, social dysfunction and somatic symptoms. Higher scores on each dimension are indicative of greater health problems. Item total correlation of each subscale ranges from 0.40 to 0.85 and the Alpha-coefficient ranges from 0.75 to 0.84.

4) *Rosenberg Self Esteem Scale:- Hindi*

The Rosenberg Self Esteem Scale, developed by Rosenberg (1965), is a self-report measure of self esteem. It has 10 items to be rated on a four point rating scale ranging from strongly agree (4) to strongly disagree (1). It has five positively worded statements and five negatively worded statements (item numbers 2, 5, 6, 8 and 9). A lower score on this scale is indicative of poor self-esteem. It is adequate for use with adolescents to older adults. For the present study Indian Adaptation of Rosenberg Self Esteem by Prashant (1988) was used for which the validity was found to be .46 and reliability was found to be .89.

5) *Impact of event Scale- Revised- Hindi*

The Revised Impact of Event Scale is a 22 items self-report measure for assessing subjective distress for any event in life. The Hindi translation of the scale was developed by Chaudhary, Sudarsanan, Srivastava, Salujha and John in Armed Forces Medical College, Pune in 2004. The responses on this scale are scored on a scale of 0 (not at all) to 4 (extremely). The test-retest correlation coefficients are .51 for avoidance subscale, .57 for intrusion subscale and .59 for hyperarousal subscale.

6) *The Face Pain Scale- Revised*

The revised Face Pain Scale was developed by Hicks, Baeyer, Spafford, van Korlaar and Goodenough (2001). It consists of six faces differing in their intensity of pain. An individual is required to indicate his/her intensity of pain by choosing a face. The responses are scored on a scale of 1-10 with higher score indicative of greater intensity of pain. However, the numeric scores are not shown to the respondents. It is suitable for use with children above 8 years of age and older adults.

7) *Social Support Survey*

For the present study the Hindi translation of Social Support Survey originally developed by Sherbourne and Stewart (1991) was used. It consists of 19 statements that are scored on a five point rating scale ranging from 1(never) to 5 (always). Low scores are indicative of poor social support. The survey focuses on perceived availability of functional social support (refers to the various functions that the different sources of support can provide). The scale was translated to Hindi by Singh, Shukla, Tiwari & Arya (2018). It has a reliability coefficient of .91.

8) *Satisfaction with Life Scale:*

The life satisfaction of the participants was assessed using Satisfaction with life scale (SLS) Developed by Diener, Emmons, Larsen, & Griffin, (1985). SLS is a 5 item scale which measure individuals' 'global cognitive judgment' (Diener, Emmons, Larsen, & Griffin, 1985) about their own life satisfaction. Items of this scale are rated on a seven point rating scale ranging from 'extremely disagree' (1) to 'extremely agree' (7). The original scale is translated and validated in many languages and for the purpose of present research the Hindi version (translated by Dr. Pooja Anand; c.f. https://eddiener.com/scales/7) of the scale was used. The SLS has been widely used in researches conducted on Indian population and is reported to have excellent psychometric properties (Diener, Emmons, Larsen, & Griffin, 1985; Burroughs and Rindfleisch, 2002).

The Qualitative Inquiry:

For the qualitative data narratives were collected with the objective to gather rich information about victims' life history, their feelings and thoughts at the time of the attack, their victimization experience and the process of recovery.

Narratives:

Narrative has been defined by Aristotle in his book *Politics* as 'a story with a beginning, middle and the end' (c.f. Martin, 1986). Bruner (2002) defines narratives as a sequence of events, occurrences and mental states with human beings as actors or

71

characters. According to Labov & Waletzky (1967) a narrative of personal experience refers to a reporting of the events of the past in a particular way. In a narrative of personal experience, the order of the sequence of independent clauses is considered to be the order of the events that are referred to in the narrative. In addition to history and literature, narratives are often utilized in research for investigating the reconstruction of reality. Narratives have been used for research in psychology, psychoanalysis, communication, women studies, gay studies, anthropology and even medicine. According to Cladinin and Connely (2000) narrative can be defined as a way to understand the experiences. Because of its ability to provide rich data, narrative research has become a popular choice among researchers. Several researchers have provided texts on narrative research (Ochs & Capps, 2001; Elliot, 2005; Plummer, 2001). Bruner (1986) emphasizes that narratives enable us to make sense of complexity and ambiguity of human life.

The narrative research has the following characteristics. Firstly, it focuses on the experiences of the individuals; secondly it focuses on the chronology of the experiences of the individual; thirdly, it focuses on reconstructing life stories by relying on active interviews and finally, it focuses on the social, cultural and situational contexts to make sense of the behaviour, decisions and experiences of the individual.

The process of narrative interview:

For the present research narrative interviews were taken focusing on victims' traumatic experiences, feelings at the time of the attack and recovery process emerged. It involved the following five phases. In the first 'preparation' phase the research questions were formulated. The second phase of 'initialization' involves

72

formulation of the initial topic for narration. During the third phase of 'main narration' the victim was not interrupted and was non-verbally encouraged to continue the story. This was followed by the 'questioning' phase during which the question of 'what happened then?' is asked. During the final phase of 'small talk' the recording was stopped and some clarifying questions were asked. Notes were made immediately after the interview.

Procedure:

Participants for this research were contacted through an NGO named Stop Acid Attacks Foundation. The informed consent was obtained from all the participants. The purpose of the research was explained to them and they were informed that the information provided by them would be kept strictly confidential and will be used only for research purposes. To maintain confidentiality of the participants, codes were assigned to them. During the first few visits, only casual conversations were had to form rapport with the participants. Once the rapport was formed the quantitative data was obtained by administering the Beck Depression Inventory, Positive and Negative Affect Schedule, General Health Questionnaire, Rosenberg Self Esteem Scale, Satisfaction with Life Scale, Impact of Event Scale– Revised, Faces Pain Scale and Social Support Survey. The narratives from the participants were collected in several sittings considering their work schedule and their willingness to talk about their life narratives focusing on their experiences of trauma and responses to the incident of acid attack.

The intervention protocol:

The rehabilitation services to these victims were provided by an external agency which was the NGO (Stop Acid Attacks Foundation). The following procedures were being followed by the NGO for the psychological rehabilitation of the victims:

Need Identification:

Psychological rehabilitation process involves use of the measures that will assist in achieving the goal of restoring an individual's psychological state to a normal level of functioning. The staff members at the NGO used to begin with identifying the individual needs of the victims. Through their interactions with these victims the NGO staff members identified several issues faced by the victims such as lack of information about laws, legal procedures, feelings of guilt and shame, self-blame and poor self-esteem. They even develop body image issues and become socially isolated because of their own anxieties and prejudiced treatment by the society. In addition, the NGO staff members also gather information about the aptitude and vocational aspirations of the victims.

The interventions:

Once the individual needs of the victims were identified the NGO staff members helped the victims to achieve the goals of psychological rehabilitation by utilizing various measures focused at improving their self-esteem and self-efficacy. By promoting the victims to participate in various fashion shows they try and focus on the body image issues. The staff members emphasized the importance of inner beauty over physical beauty. They try to improve their self-esteem and self-efficacy by making them financially independent, providing them informational support which makes them feel equipped to deal with their court cases and treatment requirements. They even try to target these issues by making sure that the victims don't cover up their faces and are accepted the way they are. The victims are also provided training by hiring special trainers based on their interests and skills. Furthermore, they try to make the victims a part of the society by promoting their interaction with social activists, politicians, celebrities, researchers and usual customers. The opening up of the café has not only provided the victims with a source of income but has also opened up avenues of social inclusion.

Various strategies that are used by the NGO working with the victims to achieve the goals of rehabilitation are following:

- **Removing shame and guilt:** The victims are provided counselling by the staff members with an emphasis on the fact that they are not the ones to be blamed. They are told that the criminals and not the innocent victims are to be held responsible for the crime. In an attempt to remove the shame and guilt the victims are encouraged to not cover their face with a cloth.

- **Enhancing self-esteem and self-efficacy:** attempts are made to enhance the victims' self-esteem by making them realize that they are brave and courageous to have dealt with their circumstances. Emphasis is laid on the fact that can achieve their life goals on their own and do not need to be dependent on others financially or otherwise. By working at the café, the victims have become financially independent. Their self-efficacy is further improved by providing them skill training based on their interest areas and aptitude. For instance, they may be given beautician training, may be made to join dance classes, tailoring classes or provided assistance in preparing for other exams etc. based on their interests. They are also encouraged to use to the term 'survivor' instead of 'victim' to give them a sense of being in control of their circumstances.

- **Providing Social Support:** The victims are provided social support so that they feel accepted and cared for. They are given informational support in the form of information about law, legal procedures, compensation provisions and health care professionals. Community social support is encouraged by promoting interactions with the customers, researchers, journalists, politicians, celebrities and other people that might frequent the café. The victims also receive social support from each other

- **Encouraging catharsis:** The victims are given a safe environment to share their stories with the staff members, other victims and other people who are willing to support the victims or share their stories to raise awareness about their needs and issues.

- **Removing Cognitive Distortions:** Attempts are made to remove cognitive distortions involving self-blame, overgeneralizations or fallacy of fairness through counselling by the staff members and awareness programs that are often held at the café.

- **Promoting Acceptance of their Victimization Experience:** Victims are encouraged to accept their victimization experience by freely talking about it and assimilating it into their sense of self. To achieve this purpose they are encouraged to identify themselves as survivors, share their stories, to focus on their inner strengths and be proud of their appearances that narrate their experiences.

Data Analysis:

Qualitative Analysis:

The analysis of quantitative data involved the computation of correlations and stepwise multiple regression. The correlations were computed to explore the degree of association between variables and the stepwise multiple regression analysis was conducted to explore the significant predictors of subjective well-being (i.e. Life Satisfaction, Positive Affectivity and Negative Affectivity).

Qualitative Analysis:

The narratives obtained from the victims were analysed using thematic content analysis. The thematic content analysis is descriptive presentation of the qualitative data which manifests its thematic content by identifying the common themes. The themes are identified by observing the patterns in the data. These themes are then used to make conclusions about the research problem. Although several approaches of thematic content analysis have been suggested in literature, the present research utilized Braun and Clarke's (2006) six step thematic content analysis approach. These six steps as described by Braun and Clarke's (2006) are following:

1) **Familiarizing with the data:** The first involves reading and rereading the entire body of data and making initial notes highlighting the manifest content of the data.

2) **Generating initial codes:** The second step involves systematically and meaningfully organizing the data. Initial codes are generated at this step which refers to breaking the data into smaller chunks of meaning.

3) **Searching the themes:** There may be some overlap in the second and third step. The third step involves examining the initial codes and identifying common patterns indicative of themes.

4) **Reviewing themes:** The preliminary themes identified in the step 3 are reviewed, modified and developed. The themes should be distinct from each other and coherent.

5) **Defining themes:** In the step 5 the themes are finally refined. The essence of each theme is identified and an emphasis is made on how each theme and subtheme is relevant to the data.

6) **Writing-up:** The final step is to write and explain the findings.

For the identification of initial codes in the data open coding method was followed. In this method the codes are not pre decided but they are identified, developed, reviewed and modified during the course of the coding and analysis process. The results of the quantitative as well as qualitative analyses are presented in chapter five.

CHAPTER- FIVE

RESULTS

RESULTS

The results of the analysis of quantitative and qualitative data are presented in this chapter in two sections. The first section presents the results of the quantitative analysis using correlations and stepwise multiple regressions and the second section present the results of the qualitative analysis of victims' narratives using thematic content analysis.

Section One: Quantitative Results

In this section the results of the quantitative analysis are presented. In order to prepare the data for analysis all the responses obtained from participants were scored as per the standard scoring methods provided in their respective scale manuals and the scores were then entered in SPSS version 20. The total scores for each scale and their dimensions were calculated in SPSS and final analyses were carried out.

The results of these analyses are presented in three parts below. The first part presents an overview of participants responses on all the variables, the second part deals with the results related correlations among study variables and the third part presents results of stepwise multiple regression analysis conducted to explore the predictors of Subjective Well-Being among Acid Attack Victims.

Part One:

Table 1: *Descriptive information of participants' responses on all the variables*

Variables	Dimensions	N	No. of Items	Score Range	Mean	SD	Min	Max
Depression	---	30	21	0-63	25.70	11.58	13	53
Satisfaction With Life	---	30	5	5-35	19.9	4.20	10	28
Positive and Negative Affect	PA	30	30	10-50	21.20	1.97	16	24
	NA	30	30	10-50	28.33	4.40	21	39
Self Esteem	---	30	30	10-40	23.13	3.03	18	28
Impact of Event	Avoidance	30	30	0-32	20.57	2.88	17	26
	Intrusive	30	30	0-28	20.93	2.72	16	24
	Hyperarousal	30	30	0-28	19.33	2.64	13	23
Social Support	Tangible Support	30	30	4-20	10.97	3.98	4	17
	Affective Support	30	30	3-15	8.10	3.22	3	13
	Positive Interaction	30	30	3-15	7.90	3.17	3	14
	Affection	30	30	9-45	27.27	16.36	9	78
	Total Social Support	30	30	19-95	54.23	24.93	19	117
General Health	Somatic Symptoms	30	30	0- 21	9.33	3.42	6	18
	Anxiety Insomnia	30	30	0- 21	12.83	3.21	8	18
	Social Dysfunction	30	30	0- 21	9.57	1.98	6	13
	Severe Depression	30	30	0- 21	11.80	4.63	6	20
	Total	30	30	0- 84	43.53	8.74	33	65
Perceived pain	---	30	30	1-10	9.67	0.76	8	10

The table one above presents an overview of the scales, its sub-scales, number of items and possible score range and the participants score range on these scales, sub-scales along with the mean and SD. It is evident from the table that the acid attack victims have scored higher on depression, negative affect and avoidance, intrusive and hyperarousal impacts of events. It is also evident from the table that the victims have scored moderately on life satisfaction, positive affect, self esteem, social support and its dimensions namely tangible support, affective support, positive interactions and affection. They have also scored moderately on general health and its dimensions namely Somatic Symptoms, Anxiety/Insomnia, Social Dysfunction and Severe Depression. It is also noteworthy to mention that participants have scored very high (minimum 8 on a 10 point scale) on pain scale which is indicative of their perceived pain due to the violent act of acid attack.

Part Two: Correlations

Table 2: *Correlations of depression, self esteem and Perceived pain with Satisfaction with life, Positive Affectivity and Negative Affectivity*

	Satisfaction with Life	Positive Affectivity	Negative Affectivity
Depression	$-.562^{**}$	.054	$.502^{**}$
Self- Esteem	$.378^{*}$	.186	-.107
Perceived pain	$-.465^{**}$	-.323	$.509^{**}$

* P< 0.05; ** P< 0.01

The table two above presents the results of Pearson product moment correlation analysis conducted to explore the degree of association of depression, self esteem and Perceived pain with the measures of subjective well being namely life satisfaction, positive affectivity and negative affectivity. The results of the analysis revealed that Depression and perceived pain are significantly and negatively correlated (r= -.562; P<0.01 & -.465; P<0.01 respectively) with life satisfaction and significantly positively correlated (r= .502; P<0.01 & .509; P<0.01 respectively) with negative affectivity. Also Self esteem is found to be significantly positively correlated (r= .378; P<0.05) with life satisfaction. No correlation of depression, self esteem and Perceived pain was found with positive affectivity.

These results indicate that the subjective wellbeing of acid attack victims is highly associated with the level of their depression and perceived pain. In particular these two variables contribute to lower levels of satisfaction with life and higher levels of negative affectivity. In addition results show that participants' self esteem is also positively correlated with life satisfaction indicating that damage to the self esteem of victims due to acid attack also impacts their satisfaction with life.

Table 3: *Correlations of the dimensions of impact of event with Satisfaction with life, Positive Affectivity and Negative Affectivity*

	Satisfaction with Life	Positive Affectivity	Negative Affectivity
Avoidance	-.103	.113	.264
Intrusive	-.469**	-.216	.463**
Hyper Arousal	-.034	.218	.443*

* P< 0.05; ** P< 0.01

The table three above presents the results of Pearson product moment correlation analysis conducted to explore the degree of association of impacts of event namely avoidance, intrusive and hyper arousal with the measures of subjective well being namely life satisfaction, positive affectivity and negative affectivity. The results of the analysis revealed that intrusive outcome of event is significantly and negatively correlated (r= -.469; P<0.01) with life satisfaction and significantly positively correlated (r= .463; P<0.01) with negative affectivity. Also hyper arousal outcome of event is significantly positively correlated (r= .443; P<0.05) with negative affectivity. No correlation of namely avoidance, intrusive and hyper arousal was found with positive affectivity.

These results indicate that the subjective wellbeing of acid attack victims is highly associated with the outcome of the acid attack. The intrusive outcome of the attack results in low life satisfaction and high negative affectivity. Hyper arousal due to the attack also results in higher levels of negative affectivity.

Table 4: *Correlations of the dimensions and total of social support with Satisfaction with life, Positive Affectivity and Negative Affectivity*

	Satisfaction with Life	Positive Affectivity	Negative Affectivity
Tangible Support	.429[*]	.476[**]	-.115
Affective Support	.452[*]	.545[**]	-.080
Positive Interaction	.442[*]	.556[**]	-.059
Affection	.264	.392[*]	-.322
Total Social Support	.356	.474[**]	-.248

* P< 0.05; ** P< 0.01

The table four above presents the results of Pearson product moment correlation analysis conducted to explore the degree of association of social support and its dimensions namely tangible support, affective support, positive interactions and affection with the measures of subjective well being namely life satisfaction, positive affectivity and negative affectivity. The results of the analysis revealed that tangible support, affective support, positive interaction dimensions of social support are significantly and positively correlated (r= .429; P<0.05; .452; P<0.05 & .442; P<0.05 respectively) with satisfaction with life. Also social support (r= .474; P<0.01) and its dimensions namely tangible support (r= .476; P<0.01), affective support (r= .545; P<0.01), positive interactions (r= .556; P<0.01) and affection (r= .392; P<0.01) are significantly and positively correlated with positive affectivity.

These results are clear indication of the importance of social support in the maintenance of the subjective well-being of acid attack victims. These results assert perceived social support especially tangible support, affective support and positive interaction are very important for the maintenance of satisfaction of life after acid attack. In addition, social support and its dimensions are equally important in the maintenance of positive affectivity.

Table 5: *Correlations of the dimensions and total of general health with Satisfaction with life, Positive Affectivity and Negative Affectivity*

	Satisfaction with Life	Positive Affectivity	Negative Affectivity
Somatic Symptoms	-.473**	.000	.670**
Anxiety/ Insomnia	-.441*	-.005	.622**
Social Dysfunction	-.304	-.552**	-.315
Severe Depression	-.338	.322	.474**
Total General Health	-.594**	.044	.670**

* P< 0.05; ** P< 0.01

The table five above presents the results of Pearson product moment correlation analysis conducted to explore the degree of association of general health and its dimensions namely somatic symptoms, anxiety/insomnia, social dysfunction, and severe depression with the measures of subjective well being namely life satisfaction, positive affectivity and negative affectivity. The results of the analysis indicated that somatic symptoms, anxiety/ insomnia and overall general health are significantly and negatively correlated (r= -.473; P<0.01; -.441; P<0.05 & -.594; P<0.01 respectively) with satisfaction with life. Also somatic symptoms, anxiety/ insomnia, severe depression and overall general health are significantly and positively correlated (r= .670; P<0.01; .622; P<0.01; .474; P<0.01 & 670; P<0.01 respectively) with negative affectivity. In addition social dysfunction dimension of social health is also found to be significantly negatively associated (r= -.552; P<0.01) with positive affectivity.

These results indicate that general health after the violent incident has significant association with subjective wellbeing. Results demonstrate that a decrease in overall general health and its dimensions in significantly linked to the decrease in life satisfaction and increase in negative affectivity. Similarly due to the social dysfunctions after the violent event people also have significant decrease in their positive affectivity.

Part Three: Stepwise Multiple Regression

Table 6: *The result of stepwise multiple regressions taking Depression, Self Esteem, and the dimensions of Impact of Event, Social Support and General Health as predictors and satisfaction with life as the criterion*

Predictors	R	R^2	R^2 CHANGE	F Change	SIG. OF F CHANGE	β	T	SIG. OF T
Somatic Symptoms	.473	.224	.224	8.060	.008	-.473	2.839	.001
Positive interactions	.664	.441	.218	10.537	.003	.467	3.246	.003
Social Dysfunction	.723	.523	.082	4.446	.045	-.318	2.109	.045

Excluded Variables: Depression, Avoidance, Intrusive, Hyperarousal, Tangible Support, Affective Support, Affection, Anxiety/Insomnia, Severe Depression, Perceived pain

Table seven above presents the results of stepwise multiple regression analysis conducted to identify the predictors of life satisfaction among victims of acid attack taking Depression, Self Esteem, and the dimensions of Impact of Event, Social Support and General Health as predictors and satisfaction with life as the criterion. The results indicate that somatic symptoms dimension of general health is the strongest predictor (β= -.473, t= 2.839, P<0.001) of positive affectivity in acid attack victims and explains 22.4 % of variance (in inverse direction as evident from the negative beta value) in life satisfaction (R^2 change= .224, F= 8.060, P<0.008). Positive interaction dimension of social support is the next predictor (β= .467, t= 3.246, P<0.003) and by contributing further 21.8 % variance in the initial variance explained by somatic symptoms, resulted in the prediction of 44.1% variance in life satisfaction (R^2 change= .221, F= 10.537, P<0.003). The final predictor of life satisfaction is social dysfunction dimension of social support (β= -.318, t= 2.109, P<0.045) which by contributing 8.2 percent variance (in inverse direction as evident from the negative beta value) in the variance explained by somatic symptoms and positive interactions, resulted in the total 52.3% variance prediction (R^2 change= .082, F= 4.446, P<0.045).

These results indicate the importance of social support and general health in the life satisfaction of acid attack victims. It is clearly demonstrated by the results that somatic symptom is very important predictor followed by positive interactions and social for life satisfaction among acid attack victims. The results thus advocate for considering somatic symptoms, positive interaction and social dysfunctions in maintaining life satisfaction among these victims.

Table 7: *The result of stepwise multiple regressions taking Depression, Self Esteem, and the dimensions of Impact of Event, Social Support and General Health as predictors and positive affectivity as the criterion*

Predictors	R	R^2	R^2 CHANGE	F Change	SIG. OF F CHANGE	β	T	SIG. OF T
Positive Interactions	.556	.309	.309	12.499	.001	.556	3.535	.001
Social Dysfunctions	.669	.447	.139	6.774	.015	-.401	2.603	.015
Affective Support	.744	.553	.106	6.182	.020	.464	2.486	.020

Excluded Variables: Depression, Avoidance, Intrusive, Hyperarousal, Tangible Support, Affection, Somatic Symptoms, Anxiety/Insomnia, Severe Depression, Perceived pain

Table seven above presents the results of stepwise multiple regression analysis conducted to identify the predictors of positive affectivity among victims of acid attack taking depression, self esteem, and the dimensions of impact of event, social support and general health as predictors and positive affectivity as the criterion. The results of the analysis show that positive interaction dimension of social support is the strongest predictor (β= .556, t= 3.535, P<0.001) of positive affectivity in acid attack victims and explains 30.9 % of variance in positive affectivity (R^2 change= .309, F= 12.499, P<0.001). Social dysfunction dimension of general health is the next predictor (β= -.401, t= 2.603, P<0.015) and by contributing further 13.9 % variance (in reverse direction as evident by negative beta value) in the initial variance explained by positive interactions, resulted in the prediction of 44.7% variance in positive affectivity (R^2 change= .139, F= 6.774, P<0.015). The final predictor of positive affectivity is affective support dimension of social support (β= .464, t= 2.486, P<0.020) which by contributing 10.6 percent variance in the variance explained by positive interactions and social dysfunction, resulted in the total 55.3% variance prediction (R^2 change= .106, F= 6.182, P<0.020).

It is, therefore, evident from the results that positive interaction and affective support dimensions of social support and social dysfunction dimension of general health are significant predictors of positive affectivity among acid attack victims. The results indicate the necessity of social support and absence of social dysfunctions in maintaining positive affectivity among these victims.

Table 8: *The result of stepwise multiple regressions taking Depression, Self Esteem, and the dimensions Impact of Event, Social Support and General Health as predictors and negative affectivity as the criterion*

Predictors	R	R^2	R^2 CHANGE	F Change	SIG. OF F CHANGE	β	T	SIG. OF T
Somatic Symptoms	.670	.449	.449	22.862	.001	.670	4.781	.001
Anxiety/ Insomnia	.777	.604	.155	10.562	.003	.427	3.250	.003
Social Dysfunction	.825	.681	.077	6.261	.019	.299	2.502	.019
Affection	.873	.762	.081	8.547	.007	-.301	2.924	.007

Excluded Variables: Depression, Avoidance, Intrusive, Hyperarousal, Tangible Support, Affective Support, Positive Interaction, Affection, Somatic Symptoms, Perceived pain

Table Eight above presents the results of stepwise multiple regression analysis conducted to identify the predictors of negative affectivity among victims of acid attack taking depression, self esteem, and the dimensions of impact of event, social support and general health as predictors and negative affectivity as the criterion. In this stepwise regression analysis the somatic symptoms dimension of general health has emerged as the strongest predictor (β= .670, t= 4.781, P<0.001) of negative affectivity in acid attack victims and explains 44.9 % of variance in nagative affectivity (R^2 change= .449, F= 22.862, P<0.001). Anxiety/ Insomnia dimension of general health has emerged as second best predictor (β= .427, t= 3.250, P<0.003) which by contributing further 15.5 % variance in the initial prediction by somatic symptoms results in the prediction of 60.4% variance in negative affectivity (R^2 change= .115, F= 10.562, P<0.003). The social dysfunction dimension of general health has emerged as the next predictor (β= .299, t= 2.502, P<0.019) and by contributing further 7.7 % variance in the variance explained by somatic symptoms and anxiety/ insomnia, resulted in the prediction of 68.1% variance (in reverse direction as evident by negative beta value) in negative affectivity (R^2 change= .681, F= 6.261, P<0.019). The final predictor of negative affectivity is found to be affection dimension of social support (β= -.301, t= 2.924, P<0.007) which by contributing 8.1 percent variance in the variance explained by somatic symptoms, anxiety/insomnia and social dysfunction, resulted in the total 76.2% variance prediction (R^2 change= .081, F= 8.547, P<0.007).

Similar to other results of stepwise regression analysis, this result also show the importance of general health and social support in predicting the negative affectivity in acid attack victims. The results clearly demonstrate that the negative affectivity in these victims is significantly predicted by their somatic symptoms and anxiety/ insomnia resulting from the traumatic event. The same is further predicted by the social dysfunction and affection dimensions of social support.

Section Two: Qualitative results

The narratives obtained from the participants were analyzed using thematic content analysis. Thematic content analysis can be done in various ways. In this research the 6 step framework as suggested by Braun and Clarke (2006) was followed. According to Braun and Clarke (2006) thematic content analysis is the process of identifying patterns in the qualitative data. These patterns are called themes. These themes are then used to say something about the research problem. In the first step of analysis, the narrative interviews were transcribed and typed in the Microsoft word document and were read and re-read in order to increase familiarity with the data. During this phase some preliminary notes were also made. One such example of these notes is:

> *The maximum focus of the victims is on the physical impact of the acid attack. The interviews instantly reveal a lot about the long term physical and even financial consequences for the victims. However, further analysis is required to uncover latent themes that may be embedded in the qualitative data. Victims also express concern over physical deformity and body image.*

The second step of the analysis involved generating initial codes which involved the organization of the qualitative data in a systematic and meaningful way by reducing it into smaller chunks. Then each segment of the data that was relevant to the research problem was coded. The open coding was used in this research which means that no pre-set codes were decided. Instead the codes were developed and modified during the coding process itself. This process was repeated again and again and in the process some new codes were also generated and some already existing codes were modified. For instance some of the early codes developed included *secondary victimization, seeking social support, objectification of women etc.*

The third step involved searching for themes. In some cases considerable overlap between the initial codes and the subsequent themes identified could be observed. For the present research the codes generated were examined and it was found that some codes fitted together in a theme. For instance initial codes like *loss of trust and violence* were collated into the initial theme of *sources of trauma.*

The fourth step involved reviewing, modifying and developing the preliminary themes previously identified. The data associated with each theme was colour coded and reviewed to assess whether it supported the respective themes. A number of changes were made during this stage and some distinct sub themes were also identified. For instance *coping* was identified as a theme distinct from *psychological rehabilitation.* The next step involved defining the themes. The aim of this step was to identify the essence of each theme i.e. to describe what each theme was about. Victims' responses upon analysis were organized broadly into five major themes with several sub themes. Even though the themes exhibit interconnectedness as well as overlapping, it enables to develop a holistic understanding of the impact of acid attack victimization and the rehabilitation process. The emergent themes and their indicators are tabulated and briefly described in the table 9. In the subsequent section the themes are described in detail with prototypical excerpts of the responses by the acid attack victims. During this phase a thematic map was also developed depicting the relation among the themes. Based on the findings the thematic map emerges as a psychological rehabilitation model for the victims of acid attack which is shown in *figure 5.* The final step of the analysis involved writing results and discussion about the findings.

Table 9: *The emergent themes, sub-themes and description emerged from the thematic content analysis*

S.No.	Themes	Sub-themes	Brief Description
1	Sources of Trauma	Embodiment	It refers to the identity of women as not being separate from their specific body form.
		Feminity	It refers to the quality of being feminine i.e. acting or behaving in ways that is typical of a girl or a woman.
		Power Dominance	It refers to the superiority of one gender over the other in terms of physical strength, authority and influence.
		Loss of Self Identity	It refers to the loss of a global understanding that a person has of oneself i.e. the loss of characteristics that one utilizes to define oneself.
		Violence	It refers to the act of aggression (acid attack and domestic violence)
		Betrayal	It refers to the damage to the trust, safety and security in any interpersonal relationship.
		Violation of civil rights	It refers to violation of one's safety, physical and mental integrity and discrimination on the basis of gender.
		Re-victimization	It refers to reoccurrence of the traumatic experience or occurrence of an additional trauma.
2	Social Support	Non Social Support	It refers to the perception that one is not cared for and will not receive any assistance or assistance in the intensity that one needs from other people.
		Positive Social	It refers to the perception that one will

		Support	be cared for and will receive assistance from other people (support from family and friends)
3	Coping	Effective Coping	
		-Emotion focused coping	It refers to altering ones emotional reaction to stressful situations to alter the experience of these situations.
		-Seize control	It refers to taking charge of one's life situations, rebuilding their equilibrium and gaining some confidence.
		-Retribution	It refers to objectively counterbalancing the injustice done to the victim by reporting the crime to the police and demanding to punish the offender.
		-Forgiveness	The processes by which the victim experiences a change in attitude and feelings towards the offender and let go of the negative feelings towards the offender.
		Ineffective coping	
		-Self-blame	It refers to the cognitive process of attributing the criminal event to oneself
		-Social Withdrawal	It refers to avoiding people and activities that were once enjoyed by the victim
		-Disengagement	It refers to the mechanism which is typically characterized by efforts directed at avoiding dealing with the stressors

4	Psychological Makeup	Adaptive	
		- Positive Life Orientation	It refers to the tendency of making positive evaluations about oneself, life and future.
		- Belief in Just World	It refers to the thought process in which the victim believes that the offender will be punished for the crime committed by him and will pay for the injustice done by him.
		- Self–efficacy	It refers to the victim's belief in her innate ability to deal with prospective situation.
		Maladaptive	
		- Cognitive Distortions o Overgeneralization o Blaming o Fallacy of Fairness	It refers to the biased ways of thinking about oneself and the world around us
		- Hopelessness	It refers to the emotion typically characterized by feelings of despair and lack of hope
		- Shame	It refers to a self-conscious emotion characterized by feelings of distress caused by some wrong or foolish behaviour.
		-Suicidal Ideation	It refers to thinking or planning one's suicide.

5	Psychological Rehabilitation	Psychological Rehabilitation Outcome	
		• Effective Rehabilitation	
		- Social Inclusiveness	It refers to the process of improving one's opportunity and ability to be a part of the society.
		- Meaning of Life	It refers to the feeling that one's existence has some significance in general.
		• Ineffective Rehabilitation	
		- Social Isolation	It refers to complete or near-complete absence of contact between the society and the individual.
		- Loss of meaning in life	It refers to the feeling that one's existence has no significance in general.

Sources of Trauma:

The term 'trauma' originates from the Greek word meaning wound. It could mean physical wound, psychological wound or both. Physical trauma can be defined as the physical injury. Psychological trauma is a subjective experience that refers to the damage to the individual's emotional and psychological stability. From the analysis of the data trauma can be described as response to perceived life threatening experiences or perceived overwhelming experiences. The sources of trauma refer to the events that cause traumatic experiences of an event. During the content analysis of the qualitative responses of the victims several sources of trauma could be identified which include embodiment, feminity, power dominance, loss of self-identity, violence, betrayal, violation of civil rights and re-victimization.

Embodiment: One's identity can serve as a strong weapon as well as a limiting factor in one's life. For males their identity is related to their work and socio-economic status. However, the identity of women is viewed as not being separate from their specific body form. This becomes a source of trauma for women in general and especially for the victims of acid attack. The idea behind acid attack as an offence is not to kill the individual but rather to objectify her and severely harm her but to leaveher to deal with painful lifelong consequences. Embodiment as major source of trauma was clearly depicted in the narratives by various participants. For instance:

> *"It seems, for him I was even worse than an animal. In fact, I was not even a living creature for him. For him I was just an object which he destroyed because he could not have it. The physical pain was immense but worse than that is this feeling that I meant nothing to him. He not only ruined my face but my entire life with it."(Participant 2)*

This embodiment of women is so farfetched that in some cases of acid attack the woman is attacked just to take revenge against the person under whose social and economic protection she was. In such cases the woman is treated as the property of the male and it is him who is being perpetrated against. Several participants indicated such forms of embodiment in their narratives.

> *"I was nowhere in the picture. Chacha had a fight with my father over ancestral property in which I or my mother had no say. It was they who had a fight. Chacha threatened my father that he would make him pay and that he would make him regret. I had no idea that he would take his revenge by attacking me. I had not even heard of acid and I was made a victim of acid attack. It was as him I was just another piece of land or worse than that which he made sure that if he could not have my father could not have it either."(Participant 5)*

"They were my neighbours. They had a fight over property with my husband. He threatened my husband that he would make him pay. At that moment in time I took that threat to be just words. People say a lot of things. They even say that they will kill each other when they are angry. But I did not think that it would amount to this. I cannot imagine how anyone can give such immense pain to a living person. It simply means that for them I was not even a human being. (Participant 19)

"He wanted to take revenge. So he thought of taking away everything from me. His idea of doing that was to attack me with acid. He thought that by destroying my face he will ruin my entire life."(Participant 20).

These narratives clearly indicate that women are often objectified as either sexual objects existing merely for the satisfaction of male desires or as property owned by males. Such embodiment dehumanizes women and leads to traumatic experiences.

Feminity: Feminity refers to the quality of being feminine. In other words, it means acting or behaving in ways that are typical of a girl or a woman. Feminity often includes qualities like submission, dependency on a male figure, coyness, subservience to needs and desires of males. However, these qualities that are described as feminine are not natural and are instead the result of social conditioning. Each woman is affected differently by the demands of feminity. These demands often result in discrimination of women, their exclusion from various social practices, non-participation in several important decisions and leaves them devoid of any social freedom. Thus, feminity becomes a source of trauma which is clearly reflected in the narratives of various participants. For example:

"I used to do everything that he used to ask me to do. He asked me not to put on lipstick. I kept them away and never used it again. He asked me not to step out of the house or even talk to my own parents on the phone.

And I agreed even to that. He was the man, the provider of the family and I was not supposed to ever question him. Once I asked him about his expenses and beat me until I fainted. So, I stopped asking after that. But he threw acid on my private parts because I dared to question his authority. He asked me to get my fetus aborted. And I refused because that was against my religion. But he expected me to consider him above Allah." (Participant 1)

"My husband used to spend all his money on drinking. But as his wife I had no say in that. My in-laws threw us out of the house because of his alcohol addiction. I begged them to at least let me stay as we had nowhere to go. And I also knew that he would blame me for everything and beat me up. But my mother in law said that a woman should always stay with her husband no matter what. So we both rented a room. He would not stop drinking so to manage the expenses I took up a job at a clothing shop against his wishes. One night he beat me up black and blue and told me that a woman who works is no less than a prostitute. So he attacked me with acid when I went for work again." (Participant 23)

"He used to work at the same shop where I was an employee. He must have been 45 years of age. I was just 22 years old. Still he kept on pestering me to accept him as my boyfriend. But how could I? I kept telling him to leave me alone. And one day he held my hand. It made me so angry that I slapped him. His ego got hurt that he was slapped by a woman in front of people. His ego got hurt that how could I reject his romantic advances. So one day while I was going back home, he came with a friend of his on a bike and threw acid on me." (Participant 9)

The narratives clearly indicate that several demands of feminity are placed on the women by their offenders and the society. As a woman they are expected to be submissive and agree to what the offender wants. They are either expected to reciprocate romantic and sexual feelings of the offender towards them or live their lives as expected by their husbands, and fulfil all their demands without questioning the male authority.

Power Dominance: Power dominance in this research emerged in form of the "superiority of one gender over the other in terms of physical strength, authority and influence". For centuries women have been considered to be subservient to men and have been treated as the second gender. Women experience oppression and sexism on a day to day basis. The culture has been constructed in such a way that women become a victim and an object of oppression. They are expected to be passive, remain under the protection of a man and lead their life according to the demands of the males. Narratives by participants indicate that the experience of such power dominance on a day to day basis becomes a source for their trauma. Moreover, sexual violence, particularly acid attack is also seen by them as a result of power dominance. For example:

> *"I did not want to get married. But if you don't get married then the society thinks that we are women of bad character. So, when my brother forced me to, I got married. As women we are always expected to adjust and we even learn to do so. But for how long can one keep up with the beatings? He would beat me every little thing. Once he beat me because the food was too salty. He would often force me to demand my brother for more dowry. I used to beg him that my brother could not afford to fulfill all his demands but then he would just beat me. Once I even tried to leave him. But my brother forced me to continue living with him since he was my husband and because the society thinks ill of divorced women. Then one day when I refused to ask for more money from my brother, he threw acid on me to teach me a lesson. He locked me up. I kept screaming and crying in pain but for two days I did not get any treatment and medicine." (Participant 7)*

"He was my sister's brother in law. He said he wanted to marry me. But I refused because I did not love him. But that made him furious. He started abusing me and fighting with me. He said that how could I think of saying no to him, of rejecting him. He threatened me that I should agree for the marriage or get ready to face the dire consequences. I thought that he would he would fight with me and my family members. I did not know that he would attack me with acid. I fail to understand how people like him develop such a strong sense of entitlement." (Participant 10)

"They call it love but they cannot even deal with rejection from a girl simply because it hurts their ego. But one does not hurt someone they love in this manner. It is not about love for them. It is about teaching us a lesson for going against them." (Participant 16)

It is evident in the narratives that acid attack is often not about killing a person but about the motivations to degrade them and dominate them. Acid attack becomes a process of intimidation by which male offenders intend to keep female victims in a perpetual state of fear. During the conversations with a regular customer at the café managed by the victims of acid attack it was observed that incidents of acid attack often serve as threatening examples for other women. One female customer shared her fears in the following words.

"I regularly come here because seeing these women has given me so much strength. But for the past few months one of the victims had been receiving threats that they would attack her and others supporting her. They were threatening her to take back the case. And today I got to know that she was attacked again yesterday. They made her drink acid. I cannot imagine how that might feel. I really don't know what to say. I feel angry and disgusted but also terribly scared. People have often seen me talking to the acid attack survivors. What if I get attacked? I am terrified to come back here. Also, it makes me think that it could have been me or any other woman. You are woman too so you know I am

trying to say. We have broken up relationships, turned down advances of several men. One cannot say yes to everyone. But there is no way to know who might get angry enough to attack us this way." (Customer)

On the basis of the above narratives it can be concluded that one of the primary motivations behind acid attack was maintenance of culturally installed power dominance of males over females and threaten to remain subservient to men.

Loss of Self-identity: Self-identity refers to a global understanding that a person has of her/his self (Sen, 2006). In other words it can be defined as the characteristics that one uses to define one self. In a nutshell, it answers the question 'Who am I?'(Sen, 2006). Self-identities enable us to construct meaning for ourselves. Self-identities are often relational. For instance, one might describe oneself as a wife, a mother, a friend. In some cases self-identities may be constructed on the basis of the work one does such as a doctor, a factory worker, a student etc. Another important aspect of our self-identity is our face. We tend to recognize each other by looking at the face. Even new born babies begin to fixate on the faces (Fantz, 1963). However the nature of acid attack is such that it destroys and damages one of the most important aspects of victims' self-identity i.e. the face. Narratives by various victims demonstrate how loss of self-identity as a consequence of acid attack becomes a source of trauma. For example:

"I had no intention of hurting him. But how could I have married a man twice my age. So I refused. What choice did I have? But he took his revenge by pouring acid on my face. I can't even describe the pain of it. He ruined my face and my entire life. I cannot go back to being the same person that I was before the attack even if I want to. I used to like dressing up. Now I hate looking at the mirror. My life has completely changed and all my plans for future have gone down the drain." (Participant 17)

"He thought that by destroying my face he will ruin my entire life. And he succeeded to a great extent. I cannot study now. No one wants to marry an acid attack victim. People get scared when they look at my face. People want to see the outer beauty. We may have inner beauty but on the surface I feel ugly."(Participant 4)

In several cases of acid attack, the incident resulted in the loss of job which is another very important aspect of one's self-identity. Often the nature of the acid attack is such that not only it destroys the previously existing self-identity but also hinders the construction of a new one. For instance, in some cases the victims not only lost their jobs because of the acid attack but also faced difficulty in finding a new one to support themselves and their family. For example:

"I used to work in the Bhojpuri film industry. I was one of the best dancers. And I wanted to work my way up and become a successful actress one day. But this acid attack changed my life. One should look beautiful to be onscreen. No one wants to see an ugly face in movies and advertisements. And it was difficult to find another job anywhere, firstly, because I did not have any other skill. And although I was willing to learn no one wanted to hire me at shops or any other place."(Participant 26)

"Luckily we found this café to fend for ourselves. But it is difficult to survive in such a little amount. But what else can we do? I tried to find a job elsewhere. But they refused to hire me and told me that all the customers will get scared."(Participant 12)

In some cases of acid attack loss of relational self-identity can also be seen. This was especially evident in the cases where the victims were attacked by their husbands and received no support from the in laws. For instance, the following narratives indicate the loss of relational self-identity as another major source of trauma.

102

"I wasn't attacked by a stranger. I was attacked by my own husband, the man for whom I left my entire family. And after the attack when I was dying in the hospital my husband and in-laws no one came to even see me. I was his wife and he just left me there as if I was a stranger whose sorrows didn't matter to him. I used to cry a lot not knowing what to do and where to go. I used to think that it was pointless to seek treatment since I had lost my family. I was no one to anyone." (Participant 1)

"It was as if I stopped being a daughter to my father after the attack. I used to cry for him. I needed him by my side but he broke all ties with me." (Participant 26)

It can be observed that victims experience loss of self-identity because of disfigurement of face, loss of jobs and relations. As a result, the victims are unable to construct meanings for themselves.

Violence: The most salient source of trauma was the violence or the acts of aggression against the participants. Interpersonal violence is found to be of two kinds, intimate partner violence and family violence. Intimate partner violence refers to violence done by intimate partners and family violence refers to violence done by the members of the family. Community violence is the violence between unrelated individuals who may or may not be acquainted. The participants of this research were victims of acid attack and their offenders were either their husbands, in laws, individuals they were acquainted to or strangers in some cases. These acts of violence resulted in severe physical and psychological trauma which is clearly observed in the narratives.

"He would beat me for every little thing. Anything and everything would make him angry. And when angry he would beat me sometimes until I would faint. He would beat me if I would ask money to manage the expenses of the house. He would beat me if he would see me talking to

anyone else outside the house. I wasn't even allowed to talk to women. He would beat me if he didn't like the food. I didn't want more kids after having three daughters. But he forced me. He used to beat me a lot. And when I got pregnant he wanted me to get the fetus aborted if it turned out to be girl child. Children are Allah's gift. That's why I refused. So he threw acid on my private parts. I didn't even know what acid was? I immediately fainted. When I was in the hospital I used to scream when they would clean my wounds. They used to clean my wounds like I was an animal with a brush. They used to clean it like one cleans a cloth and it used to smell horrible. I had no option but to bear my pregnancy with all those wounds because the place from where abortion is done was wounded."(Participant 1)

"He would come back home late at night and beat me. Every single night I was beaten for no fault of mine. He would accuse me of having an affair. Sometimes he would say that if you don't have an affair now you will end up having one. So when I took up the job he became furious. But I had no option. He was spending all the money on alcohol and I didn't want to trouble my parents. But he thought that I was having an affair with a guy where I worked. So one day when I was walking back from work he came and poured acid on my head. At first I thought he had thrown hot water on me but when it began to burn, I started screaming. My friend who was trying to help, even her hands got burnt from the acid." (Participant 23)

"I was fetching water from the village tap the next day of the fight between my father and the neighbours. I saw him standing at a distance but I ignored him. But then he suddenly came running and threw acid on my back. The pain was unimaginable. I still can't believe that someone can do such a thing over petty fight."(Participant 5)

"I was coming back from school with my friends. And suddenly two men came on a bike and threw acid on me and drove away. Neither of us could see their faces. I was just a child. I didn't know what to do. I just lay there crying and screaming. To this date I don't know who my

offender was. It bewilders me to think that someone can commit such a heinous crime without any reason. I wanted to end my life after that."(Participant 30).

Violence emerged as a major source of trauma in narratives. Victims reported being raped, beaten up and attacked with acid resulting in severe long lasting injuries.

Betrayal: Betrayal is the damage to the trust, safety and security in any interpersonal relationship. Betrayal becomes a source of trauma when a person's trust and well-being is grossly violated by the ones trusted by the victim for her survival. Betrayal may even be experienced by a person when victimized by an acquaintance or a stranger as it may shake the way they view the world. The experience of betrayal as a result of acid attack victimization can have devastating psychological consequences. Several victims of acid attack reported feeling betrayed by their offenders especially in the cases where the attacker was the husband. The following narrative by a victim vividly demonstrates betrayal as a source of trauma.

"I was attacked by my own husband. I left my family for him. I gave him my mind, body and soul. When I got married I never expected him to treat me like this. I try not to talk about it because it gives me immense pain to even think about it. I was beaten, abused and then attacked with acid. I was thrown out of the house which I decorated with my own hands. Every single strand of the table cloth was sewn by me. And in that very house I was attacked by my own husband. No one can understand how it feels to be betrayed by the ones you care about."(Participant 7)

"Even to this date I cannot believe that my own husband committed such a disgusting crime. He threw acid on my private parts. On my private parts! He was my husband. He was supposed to protect me. Instead he was the one committed this heinous crime. My body was brutally burnt. When my brother came to see me in the hospital I was lying there without clothes. Because of the burns I could not wear anything. I felt so

105

ashamed and disgusted. My husband should have been the one to protect my honour instead he was the one responsible for such a bad and shameful state of mine. I felt betrayed. He didn't even come to the hospital to see me once. I devoted my entire life to him and this was how he treated me."(Participant 7)

Although, trauma as a source of betrayal was more evident among the participants who were attacked by their husbands but it was reported by other participants as well who were attacked by their strangers. For instance:

"My parents are good people. They are very simple and so was I. I had not even heard of acid. I cannot believe that there can be such evil people too in the society. I cannot believe that one human is capable of hurting another human in this way."(Participant 28)

"Neighbours look out for each other. They help each other in times of need. Otherwise people would have lived alone. But my own neighbour attacked me with acid. We both grew up together playing the same games. But none of this seemed to matter to him."(Participant 5)

Maslow (1954) identified belongingness and love needs as one of the basic human needs. This need for intimate bonding has also been emphasized upon by Erikson (1953). But as a result of acid attack these victims felt betrayed by people they trusted and by the community and this emerged as one of the major sources of trauma.

Violation of Civil Rights: Violation of civil rights in this research refers to violation of one's safety, physical and mental integrity and discrimination on the basis of gender. The essence of human existence is in its dignified living; anything short of that has the potential of throwing human entity into the abyss of futility. However, to ensure that human existence reaches its penultimate end, artificial institutions have been created; Constitution of India is one such institution, which among other thing ensures civil liberties to all its citizens under its canopy of civility. The very essence of Constitution resonates under article 21; where 'Right to Life with Dignity' has been ensured to all the citizens as well as non-citizens. However, instances of acid attacks deprive individuals of their due respect and deter their dignity. Several narratives are not only indicative of the discrimination that the participants faced on the basis of their gender but mention that also their safety, physical and mental integrity was severely compromised by the attack and its consequent victimization. For example:

> *"As a woman we are nowhere safe. Not even within the boundaries of our homes. I was attacked by my step mother."(Participant 14)*

> *"He threw acid on my private parts. On my private parts! He was my husband. He was supposed to protect me. Instead he was the one committed this heinous crime. My body was brutally burnt. When my brother came to see me in the hospital I was lying there without clothes. Because of the burns I could not wear anything. I felt so ashamed and disgusted."(Participant 1)*

> *"I was coming back from school with my friends. And suddenly two men came on a bike and threw acid on me and drove away. Neither of us could see their faces. I was just a child. I didn't know what to do. I just lay there crying and screaming. To this date I don't know who my offender was."(Participant 30)*

The constitutional provisions provided under Article 21 entail that no person shall be deprived of life or personal liberty, all persons have the right to be free from degrading and inhuman treatment and have the right to health and health services (Singh, 2014). However, the victims' narratives are indicative of the violations of all the above mentioned rights. The psychological distress caused due to acid attack violated the physical integrity of the victims. The violence meted out to the victims and the resultant disfigurement violated their right be free from inhuman treatment.

Lastly, because of lifelong health consequences of acid attack, the right to health of the victims is also violated and these emerged as a major source of trauma in the narratives.

Re-victimization: Another major source of trauma for the participants was the re-victimization which refers to the reoccurrence of the traumatic experience or occurrence of an additional trauma. Being a victim of acid attack is tremendously traumatic in itself. Re-experiencing trauma in the same form repeatedly overtime or in some other forms is often the harsh reality for many of the victims. Several victims firstly experienced domestic violence and then became the victims of acid attacks. In several cases re-victimization occurred due to the prejudiced treatment of the society and sometimes because of repeated threats and further victimization by the offenders. Re-victimization was a recurrent theme in the narratives of several participants. For example:

> *"When my husband poured acid on me I fainted. He left me there. My daughter managed to call my father. He was the one who took me to the hospital. He was deeply saddened and angry at my husband. He thought that he would lose me and that I would die. He went out looking for my husband and did not return for long. Later brother found out that my husband and his relatives broke my father's knees. They crippled my father."(Participant 1)*

> *"The entire dispute started over property. Firstly, they raped me. Then they threatened me to not report the incident to the police. Still I decided that it is important to take an action against them. So they attacked me with a knife and threw acid on me. After the incident I got some support from the NGO and reported the incident to the police. But the police could not catch them. They continued to send threatening letters. It was clearly written in the letter that if anyone at the NGO would help me then they would attack that person and me again. They wrote that they would*

make sure that acid instead of blood flowed in my vein. But we did not take back the case. This time when I was coming back from the village they attacked me and forcibly made me drink acid. For days I fought for life in the hospital and could not speak. I can only consider myself somewhat lucky that my voice came back."(Participant 19)

"He had mixed some drug in my food and poured acid on my face while I was asleep. I woke up in tremendous pain the next morning. Because I did not see him, he was not arrested for lack of evidence. He still calls me up sometimes and says that he would like to marry me. When I looked good, was happy and was fine then he could not take care of me. What is the point of marrying him now? I told him that but he still stalks me."(Participant 26)

Thus, the above mentioned narratives indicate that the acid attack victims are often re-victimized due to the prejudiced treatment of the society and sometimes due to the threats and subsequent attacks by their perpetrators. Re-victimization emerged as major source of trauma as being victimized once is traumatic. Being victimized repeatedly further contributes to related symptoms and issues.

Social Support:

Humans are social beings and the important functions of being are social relations and social support. Social support in this research has emerged as a major theme that refers to family members, friends and other people to turn to in times of crisis and adverse life events. Social support can be of various types and is extremely helpful in providing a buffer against stressors. Social support can be majorly classified into four forms; emotional support, informational support, instrumental support and appraisal support. Expressions of care, love, trust and empathy is called emotional or non-tangible social support. Helping someone with information, advice and suggestions is called informational social support. Help in the form of some service or a tangible aid such as money, physical assistance is called instrumental social support. In the immediate aftermath of the acid attack, the victims desperately tried to seek social support. However, often they did not receive it or did not receive in the intensity that they had desired. The narratives are indicative of either being socially supported or not being supported.

Non-social Support: Non-social support is the perception that one is not cared for and will not receive any assistance or assistance in the intensity that one needs from other people. The narratives by the participants indicated the fact that they did not receive as much social support as they required in the aftermath of acid attack. For instance:

> *"It was as if I stopped being a daughter to my father after the attack. I used to cry for him. I needed him by my side but he broke all ties with me. My grandmother said that I was no longer of any use since no one would marry me and that I have brought shame to the family."(Participant 21)*

> *"After the acid attack my fiancé called off the marriage. Although, some colleagues of mine remained in touch, others stopped talking to me."(Participant 26)*

> *"Only my family members supported me. Without my father and mother I would have been dead. The people in my village used to look at me with suspicion after the acid attack. They would ask me if I had an affair with him. My friends stopped talking to me in the fear that someone might attack them as well and that people might think ill of them as well. I was even forced to drop out of school as the school authorities told me not to come. They said that the other students would get scared if they would look at my face."(Participant 25)*

The victims who are from rural areas and are not well versed with the information about the law, legal procedures and the victim compensation programs, do not know whom to approach for such information. Often they remain in oblivion of information that might benefit them or help them to deal in a better way with the situation. For example the participants reports that:

> *"I am not aware of any victim compensation program. I have not received any help or money from the government. We sold off my mother's jewelry to meet the cost of treatment." (Participant 23)*

> *"I don't know what a chargesheet is. We have filed a report with the police. We tried to follow up with them but have not received any information about the court case." (Participant 8)*

> *"My brothers paid for my treatment. They borrowed money from other people. I don't even know how much has been spent on my treatment but it must have been a huge amount. The NGO staff heard about me through media or some news article. They were the ones who informed me about the government aid. I was lucky enough that they found me and informed me. But there are so many sisters like me about whom no one knows and it is not possible for the NGO to reach each and every victim." (Participant 11)*

Narratives are also indicative that often victims of acid attack do not receive instrumental social support. For instance:

> *"After the acid attack I would manage to go for my treatment alone. My family abandoned me. No one came ahead for my help. I am grateful to the doctor who agreed to do my treatment. Before him I kept lying in the hospital for hours and no one would even touch me." (Participant 26)*

> *"My father was very old fashioned. He told me that a woman is nothing without a man in her life. But my husband used to beat me a lot. So, I finally one day decided to file for divorce. That's when he threw acid on me. After that I was abandoned by everyone. My wounds used to smell. So no one would come near me. I lived in the ruins because I had no home or a place to live. I used to beg for money and food on the streets.*

Some people would take pity on me and leave food in the ruins. But no one would listen to me. I managed the expenses for my eight operations alone by begging." (Participant 15)

From the above narratives it can be concluded that victims were often treated unsympathetically by family, friends and community resulting in familial and marital disruption. These effects were compounded by the stigma associated with acid attack and the resultant disfigurement.

Positive Social Support: Positive social support is the perception that one will be cared for and will receive assistance from other people in the times of need. In the immediate aftermath of the acid attack while many victims did not receive social support, some participants were supported by family members and very close friends. It was observed that these participants were better able to deal with their circumstances than those who did not receive such support. For instance a participant says that:

"I had stopped going out of the house after the attack. But it was my father who supported me a lot. Both my mother and father stood by my side. My father would take me for walks. He would constantly tell that I was brave and strong. Without him, I would have probably committed suicide."(Participant 30)

"My brother and his wife are the reasons that I am alive today. They were the ones who paid for my treatment and nursed me back to health. They loved me when I thought I didn't deserve it and told me that I was not to be blamed for what happened."(Participant 7)

"Earlier I used to feel really bad for myself. I knew the people in my village talked behind my back about how I might have something to do with that man. They blamed me for my victimization. But my father never blamed me. He would tell me that I should not pay heed to what others

112

said and focus on just one fact that it was not my fault. He told me that acid attack was an evil act committed by an evil person and I was not to be blamed for it."(Participant 13)

It was also evident from the narratives that the participants, who did not receive immediate support from their close friends and family members after the acid attack, did not receive support from them even years after the acid attack. On the other hand the victims who received social support from their close family members and friends continued to receive the support even years after the attack. Significant differences are also observed in the psychological well-being of such participants.

"Now most of us have recovered and have become independent. But I feel bad for some of them. I received support from my parents. But some survivors have been abandoned by their friends and family. And although, today they might laugh and are able to deal with their miseries on some days they cry. Although, one might receive the support of the world but the support of family members means much more than that. Had their families supported them, they would have felt so much better."(Participant 27)

"What happened was unfortunate. Although, today I feel happy but still crave for my father to be by my side. I keep smiling always and make others also smile. But on some days I cry for him. I wish he understood how much I needed him." (Participant 26)

Indian society lays a huge emphasis on the need to get married for various cultural, social and religious reasons. Being a collectivistic society one's identity is often tied what other people think of him or her. Consequently, the need to get married becomes ingrained among people and the inability to get married results in prejudiced treatment from the society. All the participants expressed concerns about marriage prospects. All of them expressed grief that they would not be fortunate enough to get married as they did not look beautiful. This lead to the belief, that one will not be able to receive support even in the future. For instances:

> "My grandmother keeps saying that no one will marry me now. And she is right. Everyone wants a fair and beautiful bride. People may support an acid attack survivor but no one wishes to marry her. So we are on our own for life." (Participant 29)

> "I have to save money for my sister's marriage. I know I will never get married. It is not because I don't want to but because I know that no one would want to marry me with this face. (Participant 9)

> "Most of us are not as lucky as her (one victim who got married). Don't get me wrong. I am very happy for her. At least there are few good people in the society. At least someone is happy but sometimes one feels sad for oneself. I know I will not get married. Most of us won't because we are no longer beautiful." (Participant 18)

It was however great to observe that during the course of the research three participants got married. They seemed much happier and showed better signs of coping after the marriage than they were before. Their narratives are indicative of the fact that they felt more supported and felt better about themselves after they got married. For example:

> "God gave me sadness but he also gave me immense happiness in the form of my husband. I used to feel that I was ugly. But my husband does not think so. He says I am pretty because I am a good human being. My acid attack does not bother him. He says the fact that I am happy now is more important than anything else. I feel lucky that I have someone to share my feelings with for the rest of life. He does not talk about the acid attack incident. He says that talking about it would only make me sad and that he wants to see me happy. I thank God for I am so fortunate. He always accompanies me to the hospitals for treatment. It really makes me happy and I feel that life is worth living after all." (Participant 13)

"He keeps telling me that I am not the one to be blamed. He told me that he wanted to marry me for who I am and not for the face. It means a lot. After the acid attack I had lost all hope of ever finding love but the love I received from my husband has made me stronger. Now I just want to focus on the future." (Participant 20)

"He works here at the café itself. He used to observe how I used to make other people laugh by cracking jokes. Whenever one of the survivors here would cry I would try and make them laugh. All of them have gone through so much in life that I feel that they deserve to smile now. He saw that and one asked me to marry him. I thought I was ugly and that I would never get married. So when he asked me I was really surprised. But I am really happy now. I am even pregnant. I feel complete. I feel I can deal with anything with him by my side. My family abandoned me. But then God gave me another family of own. So I am very happy now."(Participant 26)

On the basis of the above narratives it is safe to conclude that some victims received support from their family and friends after the acid attack and these victims were better able to cope. However, due to the lack of support from the community the victims found it difficult to find jobs or grooms for marriage.

Coping:

Coping can be defined as the conscious efforts one puts in resolving, managing or minimizing the stress. In other words it is the process to responding and recovering from something stressful and the process of dealing with stress or trauma and managing difficult emotions. Coping has two phases; firstly, to be able to reasonably deal with a stressful situation and secondly, to recover back to a functional state once the stressful situation is over. During the initial phases of victimization, participants depended on their conscious efforts to deal with their traumatic experiences. The outcomes of these efforts were either effective or ineffective.

Effective Coping: Effective coping in this research was observed in form of strategies and behaviours that yielded to positive outcomes and helped in improving the level of functioning of the victims. Effective coping enabled them to gain some control over their behaviour and provided psychological comfort. Effective coping helped them to thrive even in adverse situations. Post-victimization some of the participants utilized these positive strategies of emotion focused coping, seizing control, retribution and forgiveness as effective coping strategies.

Emotion focused coping: Emotion focused coping is of altering ones emotional reaction to stressful situations to alter the experience of these situations so as to minimize the negative impact of these stressful situations. Several participants reported the use of emotion focused coping which enabled them accept their situation and thus helped them to reduce the negative impact of the stressful and traumatic life event of acid attack. Narratives of several participants reveal that:

> *"Earlier I used to feel that maybe everyone else was right. That maybe I was somewhat responsible for what he did to me. But then I gradually realized and I have no reason to be ashamed. He is the one who committed the crime. He is the one who has done something wrong and he should be the one who should be ashamed. Not me." (Participant 23)*

> *"For months I used to feel angry at the man who did this to me. But then I realized that it wasn't helping. I used to be irritable and sad all the time. He did what he did and my being angry would not change that. So, I decided to let go of that anger." (Participant 22)*

It was observed that the emotional alterations made by the victims mostly included altering the feelings of guilt, shame, anger and revenge. By changing the way they feel about their situations, the victims were able to alter the experiences of these stressful situations and reasonably deal with them.

Seize Control: Seizing control refers to taking charge of one's life situations, rebuilding their equilibrium and gaining some confidence. During the initial phases of victimization the physical impact of acid attack was severe resulting in confinement to hospital and bed. So the life of the acid attack victims involved a phase of passivity and negative emotions. However, once the physical wounds began to heal some participants realized the importance of taking charge of one's own life situations and rebuilding their equilibrium. They began taking actions which were necessary to help them move on life and improve their level of functioning. For instance participants report that:

> *"I had stopped stepping out of the house. I would go out only if I had to see a doctor for the treatment. But my father would encourage me to go out and try to start reliving my life. I used to find it very difficult to roam around with people staring at me and giving me glances but I knew it was important. So, I would cover my face but made it a point to go out for some time."(Participant 30)*

> *"No matter what happens, life does not stop until you die. So I realized I had to do something because life goes on. So I started looking for a place where I could open up a beauty parlour. That was the only thing I knew. That's what I did before the victimization. I decided that I would have to restart my life and I will have to do that on my own. So, I kept trying."(Participant 3)*

> *"I broke down several times. But I never gave up. I had no money for treatment and no place to live. I had no support of any kind from anyone. But I decided that I will not let myself die like this. I used to pray for my own self. I would beg for money for the treatment. I managed everything on my own." (Participant 15)*

117

Thus, taking charge of one's life and actively taking decisions necessary to move on in life emerged as an effective coping strategy in this research.

Retribution: The retributive theory of punishment is essentially based on the ancient law of *lextalionis* or *measure for measure* from the Code of Hammurabi (Karim, Newaz & Kabir, 2017). In simpler words, it can be described as a law of 'eye for an eye'. However, in the contemporary legal aspect, the core principle of retribution is proportionality. This implies that the criminal must be punished for his wrongdoing but the punishment should be in proportion to the crime committed. The act of crime bears witness to the fact that the offender failed to value the victim as a human and violated the victim's rights. Through the retributive punishment the denied value of the victim is vindicated. This research refers retribution to objectively counterbalancing the injustice done to the victim by reporting the crime to the police and demanding to punish the offender. This is seen in the narratives to serve as an effective coping strategy for the victim for several reasons. Firstly, although the victims cannot be restored completely to a state that existed prior to the acid attack, but retributive punishment brings closure to the ordeal for the victims. Secondly, it provides a feeling of restoration of balance to the victims by removing the unethical advantage that the offender gained over the victim. Thirdly, it makes the victims feel heard. The act of acid attack made the victims feel neglected and devoid of human value. However, retributive punishment gives a voice to the victims and a sense of being valued as humans. Lastly, it gives them a sense of feeling that the offender has learned his lesson and will not victimize them or anyone else again. Retribution as an effective coping strategy for the victims is voiced in several narratives such as:

> *"They have attacked me several times. They raped me, assaulted me and finally threw acid at me so that I would take the case back. But I will not.*

*I want make sure that they pay for what they have done to me."
(Participant 19)*

*"He is in jail, paying for his sins. I used to feel so angry but this offers
some satisfaction. He deserves to be punished. I know he is my husband
but the pain he gave me was unbearable. My life has completely
changed. He is still alive in jail and does not know what the pain of acid
feels like. But at least something is better than nothing." (Participant 1)*

*"I had never gone out of the house alone. But now I go to the court on
my own. I want to make sure that he learns his lesson. Earlier I used to
feel that I should take revenge. But now it is not about revenge. He
attacked me because I said I did not love him. But it could have been
anyone else too. If I don't do anything now, he would start following
some other girl. He would attack her and ruin her life in the same way. I
have already been attacked, it would make me feel better if my
victimization can help him put behind bars."(Participant 6)*

*"I don't know who my offender was. But I do believe that people who are
capable of committing such heinous crimes should be punished. This
would set an example for other people too. And they would think twice
before ruining a girl's life."(Participant 30)*

Thus, by providing a forum for voicing the suffering of these victims and providing
them with a sense of justice, retribution also emerged as an effective coping strategy.

Forgiveness: Forgiveness is the process by which the victim experiences a change in
the attitude and feelings towards the offender and lets' go of the negative feelings
towards the offender. Forgiveness involves creating a rift between the offender and
the act of offending. In day to day life forgiveness is quite frequent and important.
However, this might not be the case in matters of crime and victimization. Very few
victims participating in the research utilized forgiveness as a coping technique.
However, those who did forgive reported that they were able to move forward and

think of themselves as survivors rather than victims. They reported that the act of crime made them feel devalued as a human. However, the act of forgiveness enabled them to establish their superiority over the offender. Forgiveness enabled the acid attack victims to think of the criminal act as an event of the past and realize that it was the time to heal and move on in life. The following narratives demonstrate how forgiveness served as an effective coping strategy.

> *"I used to feel angry. But what is the point of it? I don't know who my offender was. I don't know where he is. So it is better to let go of the harsh feelings and focus on my present. He must have done it out of some hatred. But hatred does not benefit anyone. See what it did to me. So I want to do the right thing. I have forgiven him. I just hope that one day he realizes his mistake." (Participant 30)*

> *"Revenge is not going to change my present life circumstances. My face will remain the way it is and I will have to deal with life in the same way as I am dealing in the way right now. So, there is no point in being angry at him. Only my efforts in the right direction can help me heal. That is why I have forgiven him. And surprisingly I feel much better."(Participant 4)*

> *"If I decide to exact revenge then there will be no difference between him and me. He thought I wronged him that is why he attacked me. Now, he did wrong to me but I won't do what he did. So I have decided to forgive him." (Participant 24)*

The above narratives indicate that forgiveness enabled the victims to move on in their lives by providing them a sense of superiority over the offender and by enabling them to think of the acid attack as an event of the past.

Ineffective Coping: Ineffective coping results from the use of strategies and behaviours that yield negative outcomes and fail to improve the level of functioning of an individual. Ineffective coping fails to provide psychological comfort and control over behaviour. While some of the victims utilized effective coping strategies some used ineffective coping strategies such as social withdrawal, self-blame and avoidance.

Disengagement: Disengagement was one of the commonly utilized coping strategies among victims of acid attack that was ineffective. It refers to the mechanism which is typically characterized by efforts directed at avoiding dealing with the stressors. Hence, it is also known as avoidance coping strategy in psychological literature. Disengagement could be observed as behavioural avoidance among several victims. Behavioural avoidance occurred in forms like not leaving one's house, avoiding contact from close ones, not utilizing or gathering resources required for coping etc. Such behavioural avoidance could be observed among several participants as is evident from the following narratives:

"I would avoid looking at the mirror at all costs. I had completely stopped going out of the house. And if at all I would go out, I would cover my face. My parents were supportive but I would not talk to them as well. Sometimes I would even insist on not taking the medicines as well." (Participant 9)

"My life was confined to just one route, from my house to the hospital and from the hospital back to my home. I didn't want to deal with anyone or with anything. Sometimes I would not eat the medicines. But then I would remember how much money my parents had spent on my treatment." (Participant 29)

"At times I didn't feel like even going for my court proceedings. One time I even missed the date. I used to think that my life had already been ruined so why bother for anything. So, I stopped going out. I even discontinued my education after the treatment." (Participant 18)

The above narratives indicate that disengagement brought passivity into the behaviour repertoire of the victims thus preventing them from gathering coping resources.

__Social Withdrawal:__ Social withdrawal refers to avoiding people and social activities that were once enjoyed by the victim. Several victims intentionally withdrew in their shells post victimization. Acid attack victimization not only disrupts many social activities but also results in impairment in functioning in social relationships. Not only do acid attack victims have inadequate social support because of prejudices but also, the victims themselves grossly reduce contact with friends and families. The victims often avoid social gatherings and their social functioning gets affected too. Several victims in their narratives indicated that they socially withdrew in the aftermath of the acid attack victimization. For example:

"Earlier I used to go out and often meet my friends but after the attack most of my friends stopped talking to me. They were scared that they too might get attacked if they support me. A couple of friends tried to remain in touch but then I just didn't feel like talking to anyone. I was perhaps angry with my other friends. And I took out on the ones who stayed back." (Participant 22)

"Until last year, I would not attend any family functions. Few of my cousins got married. But I just did not go. Later, I didn't even call back to wish them. I have lost touch with my colleagues too. Most of the people themselves broke ties with me and I broke ties with the rest of them." (Participant 8)

As a result of stigma and unsympathetic behaviour by the family members, friends and community, the victims sometimes intentionally withdrew socially and failed to gain from social support as a coping resource.

Self-blame: This research refers self-blame as the cognitive process of attributing the criminal event to oneself. Several victims blamed themselves for their attack. Although when asked directly whether they were responsible for their victimization, all the victims refused and said that it was the perpetrator who was to be blamed. However, most victims, in retrospect would hold their failure to control their behaviours preceding the attack as the causal factor for their acid attack victimization. Self-blame emerged as a prominent sub-theme in the narratives such as:

"I was getting late and it was getting dark so I took a shorter route. If only I had decided to take the longer route I would have been spared the horror of this heinous crime." (Participant 13)

"Maybe if I would not have slapped him he would not have attacked me."(Participant 9)

"Sometimes I think of a scenario where I would have shown courage and refused my brother to marry me off so soon. Maybe then I would not have had to go through all this."(Participant 7)

"If I would have kept on adjusting and not asked for a divorce he would not have thrown acid at me. He would have beaten me up every now and then but probably he would not have attacked me." (Participant 15)

Sometimes the victims would engage in counterfactual thinking and would draw 'if-only' inferences that had no rational causal bearing over the outcome. Such as,

"If only I would have taken a leave from work that day for whatever reason then he would not have been able to attack me." (Participant 12)

The above narratives indicate that behavioural self-blame was commonly observed in several victims which increased their psychological distress.

Psychological Make-up:

Psychological make-up in this research has emerged as a cognitive element that motivates and causes reactions. In other words it refers to a pattern of thoughts that motivate and causes an individual to react in a certain manner. Psychological makeup can be adaptive or maladaptive depending on whether it improves the functioning of an individual or not.

Adaptive Psychological Makeup: Adaptive psychological makeup is the thought pattern that improves the functioning of an individual. Adaptive psychological makeup enables an individual to take decisions and react in ways that would help them gain control over adverse situations and would help them to avoid behaviours that increase their level of stress or are harmful for them. Coping is a process and requires conscious effort. As a result of the coping process the victims tend to develop a certain psychological makeup. Victims who used effective coping strategies tend to develop an adaptive psychological makeup. Components of adaptive psychological makeup manifested by the victims participating through their narratives included positive life orientation, belief in a just world and self-efficacy.

Positive Life Orientation: Positive life orientation is the tendency of making positive evaluations about oneself, life and future.

It can be defined as an inclination to focus one's attention on the positive in any situation in a selective manner and then make sense of the reality. Victims who utilized effective coping techniques also manifested positive life orientation over time. They were able to find something positive even in the adverse circumstances existing in the aftermath of acid attack victimization. This is demonstrated in the narratives of several victims such as:

> *"I never even used to put on lipstick because he slapped me the first time he did. I did whatever he asked me to. But now I am sitting here in front of you wearing jeans. It might not be a big deal for you, but for me it means that I can finally take my own decisions."(Participant 1)*

> *"Before the acid attack I had a pretty face but no one recognized me. But this disfigured face is recognized by everyone. People know who I am and they look up to me." (Participant 4)*

> *"Had he not attacked me I would have probably continued living in the village. But today I am independent. I am working and earning in a city on my own." (Participant 5)*

Thus, the above narratives indicate that positive life orientation emerged as a subtheme of adaptive psychological makeup and reduced the psychological distress of the victims.

Belief in a Just World: Belief in the Just World refers to the thought process in which people believe that everyone gets what they deserve as the world is a just place. In this research belief in a just world emerged as a belief in which the victim believes that the offender will be punished for the crime committed by him and will pay for the injustice he has done. Victims who utilized effective coping strategies were likely to hold the belief that the world in general is just and that offender will be punished. This enables the victims to restore balance in the otherwise seemingly unjust world where they became the innocent victims. Narratives of several participants were indicative of their belief in a just world. For instance participants say:

"God sees everything. He used to beat me and made me suffer so much. But he has been punished by God. He will be punished even more by God. Today I am here taking control of my life. But he was put behind bars. When he got out on bail I felt a little angry. But I got to know from someone that his parents have thrown him out of the house and that he lost his job. He does not have any money and is under a lot of debt. He is struggling in his life." (Participant 23)

"They say that God might get a little late in serving the justice but he is always just. It is true. I suffered but he is also suffering now. He thought he would ruin my life by disfiguring my face. But look at me today. I have a loving husband and a beautiful daughter whereas he is behind bars." (Participant 13)

"Can you believe in God's grace? I was dying for the love of a man I called my husband. But he always made me suffer. He wanted me to kill my child even before he was born. I thought I would die. But I am alive and so is my son. On the other hand he does not have anyone's support. His family disowned him. And although he was not arrested then, he was arrested sometime back for some other crime. He is paying for his sins and I am living a life of comfort with my son."(Participant 1)

Thus, on the basis of the above narratives it is safe to conclude that believing in a just world reduced psychological distress of the victims as they felt that the offender was punished for the crime committed by him. This feeling seemed to restore a sense of balance and helped the victims to make sense of the world around them.

Self-efficacy: Self-efficacy is an individual's belief in his or her ability to produce effects. It can be defined as an individual's belief in his or her capabilities to positively affect their lives by producing a certain level of performance. Ability to reduce stress reactions serves as a source of developing self-efficacy. As a result of effective coping several participants were able to reduce their stress reactions. Consequently beliefs about their self-efficacy were strengthened.

126

"Earlier I was completely dependent on my husband but now I know I can do anything. I can earn and take care of my son on my own. I know I too can be something and people will know me for who I am and not as someone's wife."(Participant 1)

"I used to be very submissive. I used to think that marriage is important. But now I have realized that it is not important to have a husband to lead a life with dignity. I know I can become something without a man in my life."(Participant 23)

"I earn on my own. I am not dependent on anyone. I even participate in fashion shows. I manage my court case alone. I know I am strong and can do it." (Participant 10)

"People think that women are the weaker sex. However, now I don't believe that. I don't think a man could have survived the consequences the way I have. We are forced by the society to live in a certain way but we are not weak. I want to tell other women like me that they can be anything they want. Like me they can achieve anything they want. All they need to do is believe in themselves and not lose hope."(Participant 4)

"I have broken down several times but I have not given up. These were testing times. And now I know that I can face anything in life. I will not be defeated by the circumstances." (Participant 15)

Thus a belief in their own self-efficacy enabled the victims to gain confidence and effectively deal with their circumstances.

Maladaptive Psychological Makeup: Maladaptive psychological makeup refers to a thought pattern that would lead to behaviours that increase the level of stress of an individual and would potentially be harmful. A maladaptive psychological makeup would not contribute to gaining control over the adverse situations instead it would perpetuate stress and hinder an individual's recovery from a traumatic experience.

Those victims who used ineffective coping strategies tend to develop maladaptive psychological makeup manifested in terms of cognitive distortions, hopelessness and shame.

Cognitive Distortion: Cognitive distortions are as biased perspectives or irrational thought patterns that perpetuate psychopathological states. In simpler terms, cognitive distortions can be defined as inaccurate thinking that can cause psychological damage.

- **Overgeneralization:** This distortion occurs when an individual takes one or few instances and generalizes in over an entire pattern. Acid attack victimization and re-victimization in the same or other forms incubates feelings of powerlessness, hopelessness and one begins to think that circumstances are against them and they would never be able to deal with them. Certain victims start believing that they would always remain a victims and that the victimization experience would define them for the rest of their lives.

  "I have been raped. What could have been worse than this for a woman? But then I was acid attacked too. Now they are behind bars. But what difference does it make? If not them the society will continue to victimize me." (Participant 19)

- **Fallacy of fairness:** Fallacy of fairness results when an individual firmly believes that life is fair. Certain victims fall for fallacy of fairness and believe that they deserve to be in a state of misery because of the sins committed in previous lives. This can be observed in narratives of certain victims such as:

  "I think I must have done something wrong in my previous lives for which I am paying in this life. Maybe I am being punished

for my past sins. So what can be done? It is God's will."
(Participant 11)

These victims also report resentment when they feel that life is unfair and their offenders have not been adequately punished. For instance:

"If I would have done something wrong I paid for it by experiencing this pain, but what about him? Were my sins bigger than him? I did not hurt anyone to this extent then why did this happen to me? Nothing happened to him. He is out on bail already."(Participant 7)

- **Self-blaming:** It was observed in several narratives that the victims of acid attacks often tend to blame themselves for their plight even though the situation was not in their control. For instance:

  "I was getting late and it was getting dark so I took a shorter route. If only I had decided to take the longer route I would have been spared the horror of this heinous crime." (Participant 13)
  "If only I would have taken a leave from work that day for whatever reason then he would not have been able to attack me." (Participant 12)
  "Sometimes I think had I dealt with the situation differently, had I not objected to what he wanted then probably my life would have been better. Sometimes I feel I made mistakes and bearing the consequences of those mistakes." (Participant 2)

Thus, the above narratives indicate that these biased ways of thinking can increase psychological distress for the victims and hinder their rehabilitation process.

Hopelessness: Hopelessness refers to a state of despair and lack of hope for the future. Often victims of acid attack experience hopelessness for various aspects of their future life. Some victims would feel hopeless about finding a job, prospects of marriage or about life in general. Hopelessness in various forms is demonstrated in several narratives of various victims. For instance:

129

"I have been raped. What could have been worse than this for a woman? But then I was acid attacked too. Now they are behind bars. But what difference does it make? If not them the society will continue to victimize me." (Participant 19)

"I have to save money for my sister's marriage. I know I will never get married. It is not because I don't want to but because I know that no one would want to marry me with this face." (Participant 9)

"With the café we can barely sustain ourselves. I hardly earn anything. I have younger siblings who are still studying. Now I don't even feel like looking for jobs because I know I won't find one. No one wants to hire an ugly face as a receptionist or shopkeeper. If nothing else I know for this reason I will not be able to improve my financial condition. At least not until my brother gets a job. But that will only be possible if we can manage to pay for his education." (Participant 11)

Thus, several victims reported feeling hopeless which increased their psychological distress and prevented the victims from actively coping with their circumstances.

Shame: It refers to a self-conscious emotion characterized by feelings of distress caused by some wrong or foolish behaviour. Several victims reported feelings of shame post acid attack victimization. Acid attack victims often feel that they have lost respect as a result of victimization. Sometimes they would experience shame for behaviours that were not in their control. Some victims even reported feeling bad about filing cases against their husbands as they felt that the crime was part of their private and personal life and should have remained private. Several victims manifested shame in their narratives. For instance:

"I cannot imagine that anyone can hurt anyone to this extent. I understand that he committed a crime and should be and will be punished for it. But as a wife I feel bad. My personal life has become public. What happens between a husband and a wife should remain

*between them. I know of a survivor who still lives with her husband and
kids even though he threw acid at her face and disfigured her. Sometimes
I feel I wasn't loyal enough. But then I remember my life then, the pain of
acid melting my skin away and I convince myself to push aside this
thought. But it often creeps back in. At least I would have had a
family."(Participant 1)*

*"I really used to feel ashamed of my disfigured face. That's why I used to
cover it while going out. I was too careless back then. I should not have
taken his threats so lightly. My face has now become a reminder of my
mistakes and that is why I feel ashamed of myself."(Participant 18)*

The above narratives indicate that shame is one of the central emotional consequences
experienced by the victims and involved a strong desire to hide the damaged self from
others and a feeling of self-disapproval resulting in psychological distress.

Suicidal Ideation: One of the prominent outcomes of ineffective coping was suicidal
ideation which refers to thinking or planning ones suicide. Several victims who
engaged in ineffective coping manifested suicidal ideation which is demonstrated in
several narratives such as:

*"My parents would not leave me alone. Otherwise I would have
committed suicide. I did not wish to live. I would look for an opportunity
to be alone and put an end to my life. But then I would think of parents
and not go ahead with it." (Participant 30)*

*"Every single day I would think of killing myself. Although I never
actually tried, I used to think of killing myself so that my pain ceases and
so that my parents' money would not be wasted." (Participant 9)*

Though the victims did not commit suicide, they seemed severely depressed and
thought about ending their misery by killing oneself.

Psychological Rehabilitation:

According to the American Psychological Society (APA, n.d.), psychological rehabilitation involves the application of psychological principles for people who have disability as a result of injury or illness with the purpose of treating and assessing their emotional, cognitive and functional difficulties to improve their participation in life activities. In the narratives psychological rehabilitation has emerged as the use of measures that assist the individuals to maximal functioning in interaction with their environment and restoring them to a healthy state of psychological functioning. Following the incident of acid attack victimization, victims experience anxieties, depression, suicidal ideations, poor self-esteem, self-doubt and other mental health disturbances. The goal of psychological rehabilitation thus, is not only to restore an individual back to a psychological state that existed prior to their victimization but also to restore their psychological state to a normal level of functioning. This is achieved by removing self-doubt, anxieties and other mental health problems that may have arisen as a result of the acid attack victimization. Usually psychological rehabilitation is achieved with the help of psychologists, counsellors, other mental health professional or some other external agency. The victims participating in the present research were assisted by the NGO, Stop Acid Attack Foundation, to achieve the goals of psychological rehabilitation. The strategies followed by them in the psychological rehabilitation are discussed in detail in the method chapter.

Rehabilitation Outcomes: The outcome of psychological rehabilitation was found to result in significant improvement in the psychological functioning of the victims.

132

However, two participants who could not participate in the rehabilitation program were found to report poor psychological health.

Effective Psychological Rehabilitation Outcomes: It was observed that the psychological health of the victims participating in the present research was restored to a normal level of functioning. Enhanced self-esteem and self-efficacy was reported by the victims. They reported that they no longer felt guilt or shame. Also, they increased their participation in social activities and focused enjoying every day events of life. The victims would celebrate their birthdays and other festivals. They would crack jokes and discuss about makeup and clothes which they had previously stopped enjoying. The outcome of effective psychological rehabilitation involved a feeling of having a sense of meaning in life and social inclusiveness.

- **Social Inclusiveness:** Managing a café is a business that involves a great amount of social interaction and resulted in the expansion of the social support network of the victims along with participation is fashion shows and other awareness programs. Through the NGO the victims came in contact with other acid attack victims that enabled them to identify themselves and each other as a part of a common group. Fighting for a common cause such as the amendment of the laws pertaining to sale and purchase of acid attack further enhanced a sense of belongingness among the victims and others who support the cause.

    "All the victims here have now become my family. We laugh and cry together and share each other's sorrows and joys. We celebrate each other's birthdays and enjoy spending time with each other. Sometimes we fight like sisters but then hug it out. We always stand for each other now. We even support each other during court proceedings." (Participant 26)

133

"All of us have had a similar experience. Some have experiences far worse than mine. So we look out for each other. Take care of each other. We know what it feels like and hence all of us are demanding a change in the law together, as one voice." (Participant 30)

"Back in the village people did not like talking to an acid attack victim. But here I have received a lot of love. There are many people who understand our pain and who support our cause. They listen to us and even come for protests and awareness programs. I like talking to them. It feels good to know that people stand by us." (Participant 9)

Therefore, acknowledgement of the victims' traumatic experiences by other people helped in restoring the breach that occurred between the victims and the community and provided them opportunities to be a part of the society.

- **Meaning in Life:** Several victims tried to regain a sense of meaning in life by reconstructing their identity and assimilating their experience of victimization into it. The victims referred to themselves as 'survivors' which was active in comparison to the term 'victim' that gives a sense of passivity. This can be observed in the narratives of several victims such as the one shared below.

"I am not a victim. I am a survivor. It makes me feel like a hero. I have bravely fought with my circumstances." (Participant 4)

Also, finding a goal in life helped the victims to derive a sense from their victimization experience. With the help on Indira Gandhi National Open University's Initiative several victims took up courses as per their interest and are pursuing their higher education. Fighting for bringing amendments in the laws pertaining to acid attack, sale and purchase of acid attack has also given a sense of purpose to the victims. For example:

"I cannot change what happened with me. But if I can help others like me then I would feel that my pain was worth experiencing. I

want to fight. I want to make sure that the Government bans the
sale of acid so that no other girl has to experience what I had to go
through. I am not going to give until I achieve this." (Participant 8)

Thus, by finding a way to preserve their hope and misery the victims were able to gain a sense of meaning in life.

Ineffective Psychological Rehabilitation: One participant although worked at the café, avoided mingling with the other victims of acid attack and other people at the café. She used to pose for photographs but would not smile and would interact with others only when necessary. During a conversation she revealed that she does not enjoy talking with others as it reminded her of her acid attack incident.

"What is the point of talking to anyone? Talking is not going to help me
in anyway. I have lost my home. I was attacked by my own husband. And
I was pregnant when I was attacked. I lost my child too. Now I don't feel
like talking to anyone. Everything just reminds me of the past and it gives
me a headache." (Participant 7)

Another victim got a job elsewhere. Although, she worked in the same city she did not participate in the social activities organized at the café and lost touch with the other victims and staff members. In her narratives, such as the one below, she reported experiencing nightmares, fear of crime and negative affect even though she became financially independent and stable.

"I am glad I got the job. But I live in constant fear of being attacked
again. They have attacked me with acid twice. I know they are presently
in jail. But still, I feel scared. Sometimes I even wake up at night because
I get dreams of being attacked again. I have won the case too. But I still
don't feel good about it. I don't feel like talking. I hardly talk to my own
husband. I have no friends. I don't feel like going out or getting ready.
My economic condition is better than before but I don't like anything. I
feel I have nothing to live for, no purpose in life. So I just go to the office

and come back. That's my life. I haven't even met the other victims and
the staff at the café. Sometimes I feel that I should go. Maybe I would feel
better. But then I just don't go. Nothing can compensate for the pain that
I have gone through." (Participant 19)

Based on these narratives it can be observed that ineffective psychological rehabilitation resulted in loss of meaning in life and social isolation.

- **Loss of Meaning in Life:** Incidents of acid attack shake a victim's belief in the social order and divine order resulting into a state of existential crisis. Their schemas about safety, self, trust and attachments which allow one to make sense of the world are shattered. Events like acid attack violate the basic bodily integrity of a victim and results in violation of their autonomy. Often one makes sense of self in relation to others which gets damaged by the experience of acid attack.

- **Social Isolation:** As a result of the acid attack victimization not only do victims experience breaking of several close relations but also have to face prejudices in the society. Often the victims respond to the stressful event by further withdrawing into their shell and avoiding social interactions resulting in social isolation of the victims.

Two victims intentionally did not participate in the rehabilitation process. As a result, the breach that occurred between them and the community after the attack could not be restored. They socially withdrew and experienced loss of relational self, resulting in a sense of loss of meaning in life and became socially isolated.

Model of Psychological Rehabilitation of Acid Attack Victims:

On the basis of the results of the thematic content analysis, a thematic map depicting the ways in which these themes are interrelated also developed. This thematic map emerges as a psychological rehabilitation model for the victims of acid attack which is shown in *figure 2*. The model begins with the sources of physical and psychological trauma. The experience of trauma for these victims begins before the final act of acid attack. The sources of trauma include embodiment, feminity, power dominance, violence, betrayal, loss of identity and re-victimization. Often the victimization begins much before the final act of acid attack in the form of stalking and threats. These behaviours of the offender are embedded in the ideas of embodiment, power dominance of males over females and demands of feminity placed on the women. Often the purpose of acid attack is to convey the message that a woman is subordinate to men, her identity is limited to being an object of beauty desired by men and hence they should remain in that subservient position. Failure to do so is punished with violent acts resulting in further physical and psychological trauma. In the immediate aftermath of the acid attack the victims desperately seek social support especially from their close ones. However, while some victims may be supported by their family and friends, as a result of a culture of victim blaming and stigma in the society many other victims experience loss of personal relations. This is especially true for the victims who were attacked and then abandoned by their husbands after the acid attack. Such victims are blamed for not being the 'good wife' and are criticized for making their personal disputes public. Social support or non-social support determines the kind of coping strategy that the victims adopt. Victims who receive social support from their family and friends are more likely than to adopt effective coping strategies than those who do not receive social support.

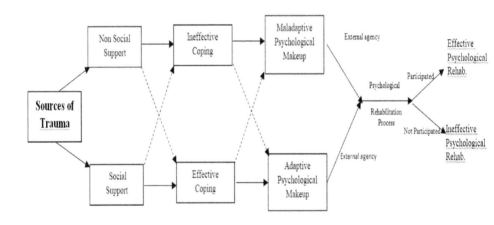

Figure 5: The model of Psychological Rehabilitation of Acid Attack Victims

Such victims are more likely to adopt ineffective coping strategies. Effective coping strategies improve the level of functioning of an individual. Effective strategies include emotion-focused coping, seizing control of one's situation, retribution and forgiveness. Emotion focused coping in cases of acid attack victims usually involves altering the feelings of guilt, shame, anger and revenge to reduce the impact of negative affect associated with the traumatic experience. After a period of being confined to hospital, bed during the initial phases after victimization, victims sometimes begin to take charge of one's own life situations and try to rebuild their equilibrium of day to day life. Some victims utilize retribution as a coping strategy which involves objectively counterbalancing the injustice done to the victim by reporting the crime to the police and demanding to punish the offender. Utilizing retribution as a coping strategy allows the victims to gain a closure for their ordeal. It provides a feeling of restoration of balance to the victims by removing the unethical advantage that the offender gained over the victim. It also benefits them by giving them a sense of being valued as humans. Lastly, it gives them a sense of feeling that the offender has learned his lesson and will not victimize them or anyone else again. Few victims may even utilize forgiveness as a coping technique by establishing their superiority over the offender and helping them to move on life by leaving the past behind. Some victims may even utilize ineffective coping techniques that fail to provide psychological comfort and control over behaviour. Such techniques are inclusive of disengagement, social withdrawal and self-blame. Disengagement involves behavioural avoidance occurred in forms like not leaving one's house, avoiding contact from close ones, not utilizing or gathering resources required for coping etc. Social withdrawal involves avoiding people and social activities that were once enjoyed by the victim. Several victims intentionally withdrew in their shells post victimization. Withdrawal following acid attack victimization not only disrupts many social activities but also results in impairment in functioning in social relationships. Often victims would blame themselves for their plight. In retrospect victims often blame their failure to control their behaviours preceding the attack as the causal factor for their acid attack victimization. One of the prominent outcomes of ineffective coping is suicidal ideation referring to thinking or planning ones suicide. It may also lead to other psychopathologies. Since coping is a process and requires conscious efforts, the choice of coping strategies further influences the development of psychological makeup. Psychological makeup refers to a pattern of thoughts that motivate and causes an individual to react in a certain manner. It can be adaptive or maladaptive depending on whether it improves the functioning of an individual or not. Victims who use effective coping strategies are more likely to develop an adaptive psychological makeup than those who use ineffective coping strategy. Components of adaptive psychological makeup include positive orientation towards life, belief in a just world and self-efficacy. Victims who utilize effective coping techniques are more likely to manifest positive life orientation over time. Such victims may find something positive even in the adverse circumstances existing in the aftermath of acid attack victimization. Victims who hold belief in a just world believe that the balance disturbed by the criminal act will be restored as the offender will be punished for his crime. As a result of effective coping victims can reduce their stress reactions. Consequently beliefs about their self-efficacy will be strengthened. Ineffective coping will increase the likelihood of developing maladaptive psychological makeup that will lead to behaviours that increase the level of stress of an individual and would potentially be harmful. Components of maladaptive psychological makeup include cognitive distortions, hopelessness and shame. Cognitive distortions include errors in thinking in the form of overgeneralizations, fallacy of fairness and blaming that can cause psychological damage. Acid attack victimization and re-victimization in the same or other forms incubates feelings of powerlessness, hopelessness and one begins to think that circumstances are against them and they would never be able to deal with them. Certain victims start believing that they would always remain a victims and that the victimization experience would define them for the rest of their lives. This overly generalized feeling is maladaptive in nature. Fallacy of fairness may result when an individual firmly believes that life is fair. Victims may fall for fallacy of fairness and believe that they deserve to be in a state of misery for the sins committed in previous lives. Victims may even blame themselves for the victimization even though they could not have controlled the situation. Another major component of maladaptive psychological makeup is hopelessness that refers to a state of despair and lack of hope for the future. Often victims of acid attack may experience hopelessness for various aspects of their future life. Some victims may feel hopeless about finding a job, prospects of marriage or about life in general. Victims may even experience shame that is characterized by feelings of distress caused by some wrong or foolish behavior. In a final attempt to attain a normal level of functioning the victims may approach an external agency. In some cases the external agency may be approached by their family members of caregivers. These external agencies are usually medical health care professional, mental health professionals or counsellors that help in achieving the goals of psychological rehabilitation. Psychological rehabilitation refers to restoring someone to a healthy state of psychological functioning. Following the incident of acid attack victimization, victims may experience anxieties, depression, suicidal ideations, poor self-esteem, self-doubt and other mental health disturbances. The goal of psychological rehabilitation is not to restore an individual back to a psychological state that existed prior to their victimization but rather to restore their psychological state to a normal level of functioning. This can be achieved by removing self-doubt, anxieties and other mental health problems that may have arisen as a result of the acid attack victimization. Psychological rehabilitation process involves use of the measures that will assist in achieving the goal of restoring an individual's psychological state to a normal level of functioning. These measures may include the following strategies; removing shame and guilt, enhancing self-esteem and self-efficacy, providing social support, promoting catharsis, removing cognitive distortions, promoting assimilation or acceptance of their victimization experience into their sense of self. This may be achieved by providing counselling, training, spreading awareness about the needs and issues of the victims and increasing involvement in social activities. The outcome of these measures will be effective psychological rehabilitation resulting in development of a sense of meaning in life and social inclusiveness. Victims may be able to develop a sense of meaning in life by assimilating their victimization experience into their reconstructed identity or by finding some other goal in life such as associating themselves to a social cause. Increasing their social interactions in different ways and spreading awareness about the issue of acid attack victims widens the social network of the victims. They results in social inclusiveness of the victims. Failure to utilize the psychological rehabilitation measure will result in perpetuation of psychological problems, loss of meaning in life and social isolation.

The above model highlights the process of psychological rehabilitation of acid attack victims and the factors that contribute in their recovery. The present model of psychological rehabilitation is a multi-resource model and outlines the importance of social support, coping mechanism and psychological makeup in the psychological rehabilitation of acid attack victims. The model takes into consideration that acid attack is an extreme stressor hence the victims would require support from external agency to help them cope with their circumstances in addition to their individual efforts. Though the model has been proposed keeping in mind the acid attack victims, considering the similarities in the impact, the model may apply to victims of other forms of sexual violence too.

CHAPTER- SIX

DISCUSSION

DISCUSSION

Greek mythology, which is one of the oldest mythologies, quotes several examples of mortal women and even powerful goddesses being ravished and subjected to sexual violence. The supreme deity Zeus abducted and performed rapes of Europa, Ganymede and Leda. The powerful goddesses Hera and Athena were also not spared and were sexually coerced. Even literature is not untouched with stories of women being forced into sexual encounters. *Tess of D'Ubervilles* by Thomas Hardy, *Rape of Lucrece* by Shakespeare and *The Colour Purple* by Alice Walker are some classic examples of depiction of sexual violence against women in fiction. These examples suggest that sexual violence against women has been existent since antiquity. However, with changes in the social conditions relatively newer forms of sexual violence have emerged such as acid attack. With its origin rooted in the Victorian Britain, mentions of acid attack incidents can be observed in fiction too. In 'The Adventure of an Illustrious Client' by Sir Arthur Conan Doyle, Kitty Winter threw acid on Baron Gruner's face, Pinkie attacked his would be captor Ida Arnold in Graham Greene's novel Brighton Rock and Harvey Dent from DC comics was also attacked by a criminal disfiguring him in the process. Although, the initial victims of acid attack in the history and even fiction were men, it acquired a gendered aspect with women now making up for more than 80 percent of the victims. Also, these few mentions do not make up for the increased number of acid attack victims who remain largely underrepresented. So, the present study was planned to understand the needs and issues of acid attack victims and to explore the psycho-social mechanisms underlying rehabilitation of acid attack victims.

The results revealed five major themes having several sub themes. Even though the themes exhibit interconnectedness as well as overlapping, they enable us to develop a holistic understanding of the impact of acid attack victimization and the rehabilitation process. The major themes that emerged after thematic content analysis of victims' narratives are, *sources of trauma, social support, coping, psychological makeup* and *psychological rehabilitation.* These findings suggest that trauma, social support, coping strategy and psychological makeup play a crucial role in the psychological rehabilitation of the acid attack victims. The analysis reveals that the severity of trauma plays an important role in mental health and subsequent psychological rehabilitation of acid attack victims. It was observed that the victims who experienced more severe trauma reported more mental health problems, more negative affect and their psychological rehabilitation process took more time than who experienced less severe trauma.

Impact of acid attack

Acid is corrosive in nature and can immediately dissolve skin. The narratives of the victims revealed that most of them suffered severe burns, partial but permanent blindness and even infections. For some victims the eyes completely melted away or were forced open by the skin contractures. The physical impact of acid attack has been reported by researchers in the past also. These studies reveal that acid can cause pulmonary disorders, swelling of throat and vomiting of blood if ingested. It may lead to formation of thick scars that leads stretching of the surrounding skin forcing the eyes and the mouth to be permanently open (Mcbroom & Wilson, 2014); Waldron et. al., 2014). Unless completely washed off with water, acid may even penetrate layers of skin and cause damage to the organs (Waldron et al., 2014). Despite the fact that physical impact has been much studied in the past researches, the psychological impact of the trauma resulting from acid attack lacks the required attention (Mcbroom & Wilson, 2014). The quantitative results of the present research also reveal that the victims suffer from high levels of depression, high negative affectivity, high affective intensity and severe impact of the event. Furthermore, the results reveal that victims' depression, intense pain, health conditions and intrusive outcomes of the event lower their level of satisfaction with life and positive affectivity. These results indicate that the subjective wellbeing of acid attack victims is highly associated with the outcome of the acid attack. The intrusive outcome of the attack results in low life satisfaction and high negative affectivity. Several victims reported that they felt like committing suicide and experienced feelings of hopelessness and self-blame. Although very few researches have explored the aftermath of acid attack, a good number of researches in the past have explored the psychological impact of traumatic events. Studies in the past have reported that perceived life threat at the time of the assault is associated with more severe PTSD symptoms (Ullman et al., 2007). Trauma has also found to be associated with disruption of psychological well-being (Sexton, 1999), depression (Brady, et. al., 2000), feelings of powerlessness (Herman, 1992), increased risk (Breslau, et. al., 1991) and symptoms of PTSD (Kessler et. al., 1999). Findings of the present research also suggest that depression and pain were associated with lower levels of life satisfaction and that somatic symptoms, anxiety/ insomnia and overall general health are significantly and negatively correlated with satisfaction with life. A good number of researches in the past support these findings. Swami et al. (2007) reported that life satisfaction is negatively associated with depression and positively with health. Also, Strine et al. (2008) reported that poor health related quality of life was associated with lower life satisfaction. It is also important to note that for acid attack victims the traumatic experience begins much in advance before the actual act of vitriolage and continues long after it. The present research has enabled identification of various non-physical and physical sources of trauma that have emerged from the narratives of the victims. These are embodiment, feminity, power dominance, loss of self-identity, violence, betrayal, violation of civil rights and re-victimization.

Sources of trauma:

Often women's identity is viewed as being limited to their specific body form. Several victims in their narratives revealed that they felt like a 'piece of land' or 'not even a human being' as a result of the acid attack victimization. An identity is a powerful tool that can serve as a source of happiness as well as a limiting factor in one's life. Identity of men is considered to be somewhat fluid as it is associated with theory, mind and abstract thought (Cahill, 2001). However, the identity of women is frequently embodied incubating the issue of constrained identity. Conclusively, women fail to persuade others to see them differently or at least more than just an object of male's sexual desire. Several victims shared that they were victimized because they did not reciprocate their offenders' romantic or sexual advances. Such sexual objectification results in animalistic dehumanization of women whereby they are viewed as no more than animals (Loughnan, Haslam & Kashima, 2009). More often the idea behind acid attack victimization is not to kill the woman but to make her life a mere experience of trauma. Narratives of the victims revealed that the offenders thought that by disfiguring the face of the victims, they will be able to 'ruin their lives'. The offender assumes that a woman is nothing more than a 'passive beauty' as her identity and utility are limited to a face. The loss or disfigurement of that face would result in the devaluation of the woman's existence. Such embodiment resulting from the focus on the appearance of the women results in mechanistic

147

dehumanization of women whereby they are viewed as a non-living object, not different from a robot (Loughnan, Haslam & Kashima, 2009). At times the embodiment of women is so far stretched that they are viewed as mere property owned by men under whose economic protection they may and are violated to exact revenge against those men.

Feminity has emerged as another major source of trauma. Women are expected to behave in a certain manner which is thought to be typical of a woman. Women are expected to be coy, docile, shy and subservient to males. Such ideas are strongly embedded in our culture as well. Manusmriti (c.f. Raman, 2009), the ancient Hindu Law expected women to be free of six demerits which are consuming liquor, sleeping for long hours, separation from husband, association with other men, rambling around and dwelling (Raman, 2009). However, Wollstonecraft (1983) repeatedly points out that much of what is defined as the feminine is just the product of centuries of social conditioning and are not reflective of a true being of a woman. Nonetheless, women are expected to adhere to them. These demands often result in discrimination of women, their exclusion from various social practices, and non-participation in several important decisions and leave them devoid of any social freedom. In a democratic society, everyone is free to participate in the decision-making process. However, women are often marginalized in decision making, as they are always taught to be feminine and play a passive role. Manusmriti lays out strict punishments for women who fail to adhere to these demands. For instance, Manusmriti suggests that in case the woman fails to meet the feminine demand of being chaste, her two fingers should be cut off and she should be made to roam around on a donkey (Raman, 2009). The narratives of several victims indicate that each woman is affected differently by the demands of feminity. Victims revealed that they were expected to be subservient to men, put up with their domestic abuse, not question any actions of their husbands and not reject the sexual advances of their offenders.

The power dominance of the masculine gender over the feminine gender is another major source of trauma. History is perpetually flagged with instances of women being enslaved by men. These result in the oppression of women and are reflected in various social practices and beliefs. Manusmriti suggests girls should remain in the custody of their father when they are children, in the custody of their husbands after marriage and in the custody of their sons when widowed (Raman, 2009). Several legal decisions such as the Sabarimala verdict by the Honourable Supreme Court resulting in plucking out of the bar on menstruating women from entering the Sabarimala temple complex to declaring Section 497 (adultery) as unconstitutional are steps in the right direction. However, they are far from washing away the power dominance that males have over women. Several attempts have been made to explain this oppression of women resulting from such gender power dominance. Sociologist Goldberg explained that a higher level of testosterone in males increases their craving for power. Some suggest that males resent the sexual power that women have over males; as a result, they feel a need to subjugate, control and dominate women to assert their power. Culturally too, females leave their paternal homes whereas men spend their lives in the same group that they were born into. Consequently, males are more closely related to a group than females. Conclusively, this gives men more power and privilege over females as relatives are likely to help each other. Narratives of several victims indicate that they were abandoned by their in-laws after being attacked by their husbands. The culture has been constructed in such a way that women become a victim and an object of oppression. They are expected to be passive, remain under the protection of a man and lead their lives according to the demands of the males. Acid

149

attack is often not about killing a person but about the motivations to degrade them and dominate them. The acid attack becomes a process of intimidation by which male offenders intend to keep female victims in a perpetual state of fear. It has been observed that incidents of acid attack serve as threatening examples for other women. Several victims revealed that they were attacked for going against the decisions of their offenders.

Violence, which is another salient source of trauma, has many forms. However, the most common manifestations of violence among victims of acid attack involve some form of interpersonal or community violence. Acid attack victims suffer from intimate partner violence, family violence and even violence from unrelated individuals. For the acid attack victims with their husbands as the perpetrators, the physical violence begins at home much before the final act of acid attack. Controlling and coercive behaviour is usually the core of domestic violence (Home Office, 2015). There is a plethora of researches indicating that domestic violence may result in several health problems such as problems in movements, bleeding, unwanted pregnancies, weight loss, miscarriage etc. among several others (Kapoor, 2000; Naved, 2013; Semahegn & Mengistie, 2015). Past researches also indicate that women victims of domestic violence often suffer from a symptom complex called Battered Women Syndrome (Walker, 1984). Symptoms of Battered Women Syndrome (BWS) are similar to the symptoms of PTSD and involve feelings of depression, anxiety, hopelessness, isolation, sleep disturbances, intrusive thoughts and feelings about the abuse, among other symptoms. In many cases, domestic violence may culminate into the act of acid attack. In majority cases of acid attack, the victims are usually acquainted with their perpetrators. The severity of the physical impact of acid attack depends on its concentration level and also on the duration of its contact with the tissue. According to Mannan et al. (2007), the psychosocial impact of vitriolage is grossly underreported. Findings of their research indicated that individuals who had experienced acid attack manifested high levels of psychological distress. Psychological correlates of acid attack include self-blame, fear of rejection, body image issues, anxiety disorders and depression, among others which support the findings of the present research.

Acid attack results in loss of identity which becomes yet another source of trauma. Sen (2006) advocated that identity can serve as a powerful weapon as it typically answers the question "Who am I". Self-identity is often relational or contextual. Due to marital and familial disruption as consequence of acid attack, several acid attack victims experienced loss of relational identity. Victims report feeling that they 'cannot go back to being the same person' or they stopped being a 'daughter to the father'. Also, as a result of loss of job and inability to find a new one, victims experience loss of identity. Face of an individual is an important aspect of one's self identity. People tend to recognize each other by looking at their faces. The nature of acid attack is such that it disfigures the face and damages one of the most important aspects of self-identity. Erikson (1953) defined identity as a sense of continuity and personal sameness across situations. However, sudden loss of job, relations and face results in disruption of this continuity and the identity gets bifurcated into before and after. Moreover, after the experience of acid attack victimization, the individual may get labelled as a 'victim' thus restraining their identity solely to the experience of acid attack. This results in lack of linguistic options available to the victims to describe their identities after the victimization (Mittal & Singh, 2018). Constrained identity resulting as a result of making the traumatic event central to one's self-identity becomes a source of trauma. Boals & Schuettier (2011) also reported that construing the trauma as central to one's identity leads to an increase in the symptoms of PTSD.

Another major source of trauma that emerged in the narratives of the victims was betrayal which can have devastating psychological consequences. Although the feeling of betrayal is experienced even when attacked by strangers, the feeling is more intense in cases where the perpetrator is related to the victims. Narratives of several victims reveal how they felt betrayed because they were attacked by their husbands who was 'supposed to protect' them. Betrayal may shatter the sense of connection between the community and the individual resulting in a crisis of faith (Herman, 1992). One major outcome of betrayal is permeated distrust of the community (Lifton, 1973). Past researches also indicate that the effects of betrayal are inclusive of self-doubt, damaged self-esteem, feelings of shock, anger and grief (Rachman, 2010). Narratives of the victims indicate that they felt ashamed, disgusted, depressed, angry and even shocked by the betrayal resulting from acid attack.

The Article 21 of the Indian constitution requires the Government to protect the right to life. Acid attack is a severe violation of right to life as several times the initial acid attack itself proves fatal. In other cases, the victims may die as a result of resulting medical complications and even suicide (Haque & Ahsan, 2014). Acid attack causes severe injuries. As a result victims may require lifelong treatment and medical assistance. Several victims revealed that they did not receive immediate medical care and also reported lack of access to mental health professionals after the attack which is severe violation of their right to health. Article 7 of ICCPR (International Covenant on Civil and Political Rights) which was signed by India in 1968, requires India to protect all her people from any kind of cruelty, torture or inhuman treatment (McBroom, 2014). The drastic physical impact of acid attack creates life-long challenges for the victims there by involving a direct violation of the above article. Convention on the Elimination of all forms of Discrimination against Women (CEDAW), which was signed by India in 1993, requires India to shield her women from any kind of gender based discrimination (McBroom, 2014). The gendered aspect of acid attacks in India is clearly indicative of violation of the above convention. As a result of such violation, victims face several challenges such as social exclusion, psychological disruption and long term physical consequences. Findings of research by Johnston et al. (2009) emphasize that Human Rights violations are associated with psychological health impact.

Re-victimization has also emerged as a major source of trauma. Ruback, Clark and Warner (2014) suggest that violent criminal victimization leads to several behavioural changes that further increase the risk of re-victimization. Re-victimization is a harsh reality for many victims as they are often re-attacked or threatened by the offender. Victims revealed that many of them are threatened to not take a legal action against the offender to spare themselves of 'dire consequences'. Many victims of acid attack usually report having been victims of stalking, domestic violence, physical assault and sometimes even rape. Researches in the past have reported a strong link between re-victimization and emotion regulation difficulties (Walsh, DiLillo & Scalora, 2011). Re-victimized women have also been found to be more likely than women victimized once to have a lifetime diagnosis of post-traumatic stress disorder (Arata, 1991). Moreover, victims may experience secondary victimization at the hands of the criminal justice system, prejudiced treatment by the society, stigmatization and culture of victim blaming. Secondary victimization too, is associated with the development of severe trauma symptoms (Garvin &LeClair, 2013). Re-victimization can be reduced significantly if the victims are satisfied with the police and victim specialists and that victim compensation is a step in that direction (Mummert, 2014). However, often, victims are not aware of the laws, legal procedures, medical provisions and compensation schemes.

Social Correlates of Acid Attack Victimization:

Humans are social beings hence it is in their nature to seek forming close and committed relationship with others people. Erikson (1959) emphasized on the fact that it is crucial for people to develop close relations with other people to experience intimacy. Failure to do so results in feelings of loneliness and isolation. This may lead to resurfacing of insecurities and self-harming tendencies in addition to other psychological problems. One important function of social relations is social support. Social support has emerged as a major theme during content analysis and findings suggest that it has powerful influences on psychological health and rehabilitation outcomes for the victims. At the time of the acid attack many victims do not receive assistance from other people because until completely washed off it will burn the hands of anyone who touches the victim. In the aftermath of acid attack the victims are vulnerable and seek social support to share their loss and receive fairness and compassion. Herman (1992) emphasized that acknowledgement of the traumatic event by other people helps in restoring the breach between the victim and the community and helps them to mourn. Incomplete mourning on the other hand would result in entrapment in the trauma (Lifton, 1973). A good number of studies in the past have emphasized the importance of social support in recovery from trauma. Burgess and Holmstrom (1979) reported that women having a stable relationship with a partner recovered faster than those women who did not have such a relationship. However, often the society fails to view the attack as a violation and instead blames the victim resulting in familial and marital disruption. Mcbroom and Wilson (2014) reported that disfigurement as a result acid attack reduces the opportunity of these victims to get married and those who are married at the time of the attack are often abandoned by their husbands. Also, often victims have to face the prejudiced treatment by the society because of their scarred and disfigured appearance.

It is evident from the quantitative results that positive interaction and affective support dimensions of social support and social dysfunction dimension of general health are significant predictors of positive affectivity among acid attack victims. The results indicate the necessity of social support and absence of social dysfunctions in maintaining life satisfaction among these victims. MacGregor et al. (1953) was among the pioneers to discuss the serious psycho-social difficulties that are faced by the facially deformed patients. In a later study, Goffman (1963) highlighted how facial deformity could lead to stigmatization of individuals. Negative reactions to facial disfigurements of acid attack victims are further strengthened by the social conditioning of sinister beliefs that link facial disfigurements to evil. For instance, Harvey Dent who is character from the DC comics was an upright district attorney of the city and fought for justice. However, once his face was disfigured by a criminal with the use of vitriol and thus he became a criminal mastermind.

The other results of the quantitative analysis reveal that tangible support, affective support, positive interaction dimensions of social support are significantly and positively correlated with life satisfaction and positive affectivity. Various researches have stressed the importance of social support in the coping and improving the functioning of the individuals after the occurrence of traumatic events (Sarason, Sarason & Pierce, 1995; Thoits, 1986; Gore, 1985). It has also been reported that after a traumatic experience such as rape, the discussion about the same with supportive others helps the victims to reform positive assumptions about the world, explore the personal meaning of the experience and gain control over their emotions (Janoff-Bulman, 1992; Pennebaker et al., 1990).

Coping with Acid Attack:

Coping always occurs in the context of perceived stressful life events. The conscious efforts can be effective or ineffective. The findings of the present research indicate that victims of the acid attack who received social support from their family and friends are more likely to engage in effective coping strategies than those who do not receive social support. Effective coping strategies usually utilized by the victims of the acid attack include emotion-focused coping, seizing control, retribution and forgiveness. Several acid attack victims utilize emotion-focused coping, which enables them to accept their situation and thus helps them to reduce the negative impact of the stressful and traumatic life event of acid attack. It was observed that the emotional alterations made by the participants mostly included altering feelings of guilt, shame, anger and revenge. Narratives of the victims reveal that many of them altered their feelings of shame by believing that 'it should be the offender who should be ashamed' and that their 'anger would not change anything and so it is better to let go'. In some cases, the distressing phase of post victimization was viewed as a challenge that needed to be overcome by any means. Similar findings were also reported by Lipowski (1970) that many patients of serious illnesses viewed the illness as a challenge that needed to be defeated. A similar phenomenon was reported among cancer patients by Moos (1986). Several other pieces of research also offer support for the effectiveness of emotion-focused coping (Green, Choi, & Kane, 2010; Silver &Wortman, 1980).

Another effective coping strategy utilized by the victims of acid attack was seizing control. During the initial phases of victimization, the physical impact of acid attack tends to be severe, resulting in confinement to hospital and bed. So the life of the acid attack victims is blighted by a phase of passivity and negative emotions. Several pieces of research in the past have reported that victims of crime often experience a feeling of loss of control (Grabosky, 1989; Kilpatrick et al., 1989). Victims of acid attack too experience a loss of control at the time of the event. This feeling of lack of control over life situations may be experienced even after the event. However, once the physical wounds begin to heal victims may begin to take charge of their life situations and rebuild their equilibrium. Victims revealed in their narratives that they realized the need to do something as life goes on. They begin taking actions necessary to help them move on in life and improve their level of functioning. Restoring their sense of control helps the victims to cope. Friedman (1985) reported that proper response, assistance and counselling could enhance a victim's sense of control.

Retribution emerged as another effective coping strategy in the narratives which is loosely described as law of 'eye for an eye'. However, in reality, no one assumes that an acid attack offender must also be attacked with acid. Instead, moral equivalence is established between crimes and the permissible punishments. Victims revealed in their narratives that they wanted to make sure that the offender 'learnt a lesson', 'paid for his sins' and 'would not attack anyone else'. The tendency to seek retribution or retaliate is ingrained in human nature at psychological, biological and cultural levels. Similar behaviour can be viewed in primates too (Silk, 1992). Retribution helps the victims to feel better by restoring a sense of balance. Such victim centric supportive arguments for retribution have also been given by several other theorists such as Hegel (1952), Herbert Morris (1968), Norval Morris (1974) and Fletcher (1999).

Another effective coping strategy sometimes utilized by the victims of acid attacks is the act of forgiveness. The concept of forgiveness is thousands of years old and is deeply rooted in religious, theoretical and philosophical perspectives. Murphy and Hampton (1988) asserted that forgiveness is concerned with how one feels about someone and fundamentally involves a change in feelings. Forgiveness involves creating a rift between the offender and the act of offending. Narratives of victims revealed that they forgave the offender because deciding to exact revenge would not leave any difference between them and the offender. They reported that the act of crime made them feel devalued as a human. However, the act of forgiveness enabled them to establish their superiority over the offender. Also, it was observed that victims forgave the offenders without showing mercy, which refers to remitting punishment out of mercy. Bibas (2007) also reported that victims could sometimes forgive without recommending mercy. Victims shared that though they had forgiven the offender they were still fighting the case because vitriolage is a crime and it is important to ensure safety of other girls. Victims who forgave their offenders reported that they were able to move forward and think of themselves as survivors rather than victims. Forgiveness enabled the acid attack victims to think of the criminal act as an event of the past and realize that it was the time to heal and move on in life. In the past several pieces of research have established a link between forgiveness and mental health benefits including a reduction in symptoms of depression, lower levels of anger, state anxiety and stress in addition to enhanced positive relational health (Berry & Worthington, 2001; Worthington, 2005; Worthington & Drinkard, 2000). Raj, Elizabeth & Padmakumari (2016) also reported that forgiveness results incompetence to deal with challenges, improved self-acceptance and well-being. Seybold et al. (2001) and Krause & Ellison (2003) also emphasized that forgives leads to positive

158

mental health outcomes. Freedman & Enright (1996) also reported that an increase in the measures of forgiveness was related to a decrease in the levels of anxiety and depression among victims of incest.

As mentioned previously, findings of the present research suggest that lack of social support among victims of acid attack was found to be associated with utilizing ineffective coping strategies that include self-blame, social withdrawal and disengagement. When asked directly whether they were responsible for their victimization, all the victims refused and said that it was the perpetrator who was to be blamed. Nonetheless, in retrospect, most of them shared that giving into the demands of the perpetrator, not resisting, accepting his sexual advances or choosing and alternative route back to home from office could have helped in avoiding the attack. Several other pieces of research provide evidence for the link between self-blame and depression (Hamberg, Hamberg & deGoza, 1953; West & Shuck, 1978). However, it was observed that with proper social support and use of rehabilitation measures, several victims stopped blaming themselves, following which they reported better mental health. Brickman et al. (1982) also reported that victims could adapt better if they hold themselves responsible for resolving the problem and not blame themselves for the undesirable event. Another ineffective coping strategy frequently utilized by the victims of acid attack was social withdrawal. Acid attack results in disruption of social relations. Society unjustifiably values physical attractiveness (Shaw, 1981). Goffman (1963) also emphasized that disfigurement stigmatizes. Consequently, victims do not receive adequate social support and are discriminated against. Also, acid attack is usually committed by someone known to the victims such husbands, colleagues or neighbours and causes the victims to feel extreme betrayal. The victims themselves grossly reduce contact with friends and families. Gutner,

Rizvi, Monson and Resick (2006) reported that victims of violent crimes who know their perpetrators are more likely to socially withdraw in an attempt to cope than those attacked by a stranger. Victims reported avoiding family functions, public places, restricting their lives to home and hospital visits and become socially isolated which has potentially harmful physical and mental health effects on mental and general health. Findings of the present research reveal that due to the social dysfunctions after the violent event people also have significant decrease in their positive affectivity. Yasamy, Dua, Harper and Saxena (2010) reported that social isolation could have adverse effects on mental and general health. Cruces et al. (2014) also reported that social isolation had been found to harm neural, endocrine and immune levels that can lead to several other pathologies. Another similar ineffective coping strategy utilized by the victims of acid attack was disengagement. Several victims revealed in their narratives that they would avoid social gatherings, avoid meeting their closed ones, would avoid going out of the house, would avoid going to their court proceedings and avoid gathering resources required for coping. Several studies stress the preventive role of avoidance coping in recovery (Foa & Kozak, 1986; Ehlers & Clark, 2000; Resick, 2001). Increased PTSD symptomatology has also been found to be associated with avoidance coping strategy after various traumatic events (Bryant & Harvey, 1995), including sexual assault (Gibson & Lietenberg, 2001). It was also found that those acid attack victims who utilized effective coping strategies were more likely to have an adaptive psychological makeup than those who utilized ineffective coping strategies.

Psychological makeup and coping with acid attack

Adaptive psychological makeup enables an individual to make decisions and react in ways that would help them gain control over adverse situations and would help them to avoid behaviours that increase their level of stress or are harmful to them. Components of adaptive psychological makeup manifested by the victims participating in the research included positive life orientation, belief in a just world and self-efficacy. Victims who utilized effective coping techniques also manifested positive life orientation over time. They were able to find something positive even in the adverse circumstances existing in the aftermath of acid attack victimization. Several participants revealed in their narratives that earlier they were dependent on their husbands but became independent and empowered after their attack and were free to take their own decisions. Past researches have related positive life orientation to optimism, emotional vitality and emotional well-being (Agarwal, Dalal, Agarwal & Agarwal, 1995; Pitkala, Laakkonen, Strandberg & Tilvis 2004). Fagerstrom (2010) has also stressed the importance of positive life orientation as the inner health resource. Another component of adaptive psychological makeup is the belief in a just world which enables the victims to restore balance in the otherwise seemingly unjust world where they became innocent victims. Victims reported feeling that the offender will be punished by God and that he would suffer for the crime committed by him. Belief in a just world also leads to justice driven reactions and is associated with subjective well-being (Dalbert, 2001). Victims reported that they believed in the criminal justice system which would ensure punishment to the offenders. According to some researchers, (i.e. Messick et al., 1985; Lerner, 1980) belief in just world lead to an optimistic outlook of the future. Findings of the research by Bulman & Wortman (1977) also suggest that victims of aggression who believe in a just world report more positive affect than those who do not believe in a just world. Jiang et al. (2015) also reported that belief in just world has also been found to reduce depressive symptoms. Self-efficacy is another major component of the psychological makeup of acid attack

161

victims. After victimization, the victims may experience hopelessness, helplessness and lower levels of self-efficacy. Findings of research conducted in the past indicate that various forms of victimization are associated with lower levels of self-efficacy (Benight & Bandura, 2004; Frinkelhor & Browne, 1985). Ability to reduce stress reactions serves as a source of developing self-efficacy. As a result of effective coping several acid attacks, victims were able to reduce their stress reactions. Consequently, beliefs about their self-efficacy were strengthened. Victims revealed in their narratives that they felt that they could succeed without a man in their life, take care of themselves and their loved ones on their own. Past researches indicate that a higher level of self-efficacy enables people to perceive threatening situations as significant challenges resulting in lesser levels of stress (Bandura, 1997). Also, researches indicate that high levels of self-efficacy are associated with better mental health (Kim, 2003; Bandura, 1988; Muris, 2002).

Components of maladaptive psychological makeup manifested by the acid attack victims participating in the research included cognitive distortions, hopelessness, suicidal ideation and shame. Abdullah, Saleh, Mahmud and Ghani (2011) too reported that victims of sexual violence might have a certain level of cognitive distortions, which results in hopelessness, helplessness and self-criticism. They also reported that self-criticism was found to be a predictor of depression. The Quantitative findings of the research show that victims have scored high on depression and negative affectivity. Also, victims scored very high on affect intensity measured by Faces Pain Scale. Researches in the past have established pain as a consistent risk factor for suicidal thoughts (Calati, Bakhiyi, Artero, Ilgen&Courtet, 2015). Also, Carlton & Daene (2000) reported that suicidal ideation is associated with lower help seeking intentions. Three types of cognitive distortions commonly observed among victims of acid attack are the fallacy of fairness, overgeneralization and blaming. Certain acid attack victims fall for the fallacy of fairness and believe that they deserve to be in a state of misery because of the sins committed in previous lives. These victims also report resentment when they feel that life is unfair, and their offenders have not been adequately punished. It was also observed that the victims of acid attacks often tend to blame themselves for their plight even though the situation was not in their control. Owen and Chard (2001) reported that victims of sexual abuse tend to focus on self-blame attributions. Findings of research by Branscombe et al. (2003) suggest that blaming oneself leads to greater distress among rape victims. Acid attack victimization and re-victimization in the same or other forms incubates feelings of powerlessness, hopelessness and these feelings are often overgeneralized by the victims. Victims shared that if not the offender, they would continue to be victimized by the society. Hence, victims start believing that they would always remain a victim and that the victimization experience would define them for the rest of their lives. Findings of past researches indicate that various cognitive distortions have been found to have adverse effects of mental health and recovery. Owen and Chard (2001) found an association between cognitive distortions and increased PTSD symptoms among rape victims. Beck (1963) stressed the role of cognitive distortions in increasing the symptoms of depression. Weishaar (1996) has also linked cognitive distortions to increased suicide risk. Often victims of acid attack experience hopelessness for various aspects of their future life. Some victims would feel hopeless about finding a job, prospects of marriage or about life in general. Hopelessness is often the outcome of cognitive distortions and in itself is associated with several negative influences on mental health. Beck, Kovac & Weissman (1975) reported a link between hopelessness and depression. Minkoff, Bergman, Beck & Beck (2006) reported that hopelessness

163

increases depression symptoms and increases suicide risk. Beck & Weishaar (1992) also emphasized that hopelessness is associated with poor problem-solving skills and leads to depression and increased suicide risk. Maladaptive psychological makeup was also manifested in the form of shame. Acid attack victims often feel that they have lost respect as a result of victimization. Sometimes they would experience shame for behaviours that were not in their control. Some victims even reported feeling bad about filing cases against their husbands as they felt that the crime was part of their private and personal life and should have remained private. This also tends to explain why victims often do not report the crime initially and often continue to stay with their offenders until things get out of hands. In the past several studies have explored the reasons why victims stay with their abusers (Meyer, 2012; Rhode & McKenzie, 1998). Gilbert and Sanghera (2004) reported that Asian women believe that their actions can bring shame and honour to the family. They also reported that the importance of maintaining the honour of the family was also associated with personal shame, which leads to their entrapment in difficult relationships. Shame has also been found to have an adverse influence on mental health according to the findings of several studies. Uji, Shikai, Shono and Kitamura (2007) reported that shame was a direct predictor of PTSD among women with negative sexual experiences. In another study, shame was found to be a moderator between victimization and various mental health symptoms (Shorey et al., 2010).

Psychological Rehabilitation

The findings of the present research suggest that victims with maladaptive psychological makeup were less likely to seek help from an external agency. Due to lack of access to mental health professional and mental health facilities, the staff members of the NGO helped the victims to achieve the rehabilitation goals by utilizing several measures such as enhancing their self-esteem and self-efficacy, removing cognitive distortions, providing social support including informational social support, emotional, social support and instrumental social support, promoting catharsis and acceptance of their victimization experience. Participation of the victims in the psychological rehabilitation process resulted in effective psychological rehabilitation with social inclusiveness and a sense of meaning in life as outcome. Non-participation in the psychological rehabilitation process by two victims resulted in ineffective psychological rehabilitation manifested as social isolation and loss of meaning in life. Support for the effectiveness of the measures utilized by NGO staff for the psychological rehabilitation of acid attack victims comes from various studies carried out in the past. Janet (c.f. Herman, 1992) asserted that assimilation of acceptance of traumatic experience leads to a feeling of triumph among victims. Janet also emphasized the importance of restoring a sense of self-efficacy to reduce feelings of helplessness. According to Flannery (1990), the shattered sense of self of a victim can be rebuilt through social support, which may take various forms and may change during the resolution of trauma. Herman (1992), in her book 'Trauma and Recovery', reported that victims need social support to overcome cognitive distortions of shame and guilt. Herman (1992) further emphasized that sharing of traumatic experiences with other people is a precondition for restoring a sense of the meaningful world.

Based on the relationship between the themes that emerged after the analysis of the qualitative data a model of psychological rehabilitation is proposed for the acid attack victims. The present research utilizes the psycho-social-coping theory proposed by Dussich (1985). The theory suggests that it is important to utilize whatever resources available to the victim to cope after a traumatic experience. The model of psychological rehabilitation proposed in the current research too emphasizes on the role of different resources in the ultimate goal of psychological rehabilitation such as social support, coping mechanism and psychological rehabilitation. However, the current model is better suited to understand psychological rehabilitation process of acid attack victims for various reasons. Firstly, the model proposed by Dussich (1985) is a coping model, and the present research proposes a psychological rehabilitation model. Coping involves personal conscious efforts to deal with stressors, whereas psychological rehabilitation involves an external agency helping the victims in identifying the issues, weaknesses and strengths and overcoming the stressors. In reality, in the face of an extreme stressor such as an acid attack, victims are unable to cope solely through their efforts and do seek help from an external agency. This has not been taken into consideration by the psycho-social-coping model. Secondly, Dussich's model talks about four phases of coping. The first phase begins with the awareness that a problem may emerge. The second phase is known as the preparation phase. This involves awareness of the fact that the problem is impending. This awareness will lead to the person worrying, appraising, practising and rehearsing. This behaviour might lead to success. The third phase occurs when the problem presents itself. The individual may be able to cope successfully in the face of the problem if they can utilize learned resourcefulness, self-delivered reassurance and diminished vulnerability. On the other hand, the individual will fail to cope due to learned helplessness, increased vulnerability and disappointment. In reality, no amount of practising, appraising and rehearsing may prepare an individual for an event as traumatic as an acid attack. Lastly, the fourth phase is the phase of reappraisal, which commences when the problem ends. During the fourth phase, secondary coping occurs, which leads to successful coping. Absence of secondary coping will lead to failure to cope. However, in the case of an acid attack victim, complete recovery does not occur. Their physical injuries are severe and may even last a lifetime. Moreover, their faces become reminders of their traumatic experiences. So, the model of psychological rehabilitation of acid attack victims emphasizes effective psychological rehabilitation which concerned with ensuring that the issues of acid attack victims come with manageable limits.

CPSIA information can be obtained
at www.ICGtesting.com
Printed in the USA
BVHW072116120223
658291BV00014B/2105